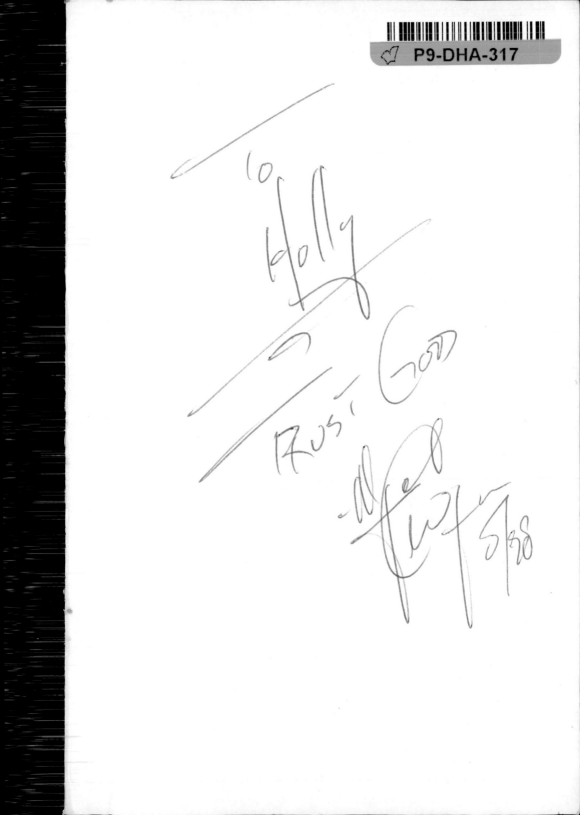

To
Holly

Trust God

TEST OF FAITH

MYCHAL WYNN

M Y C H A L   W Y N N

TEST OF FAITH

**A PERSONAL TESTIMONY OF
GOD'S GRACE, MERCY, AND
OMNIPOTENT POWER**

Rising Sun Publishing
(800) 524-2813

TEST OF FAITH

ISBN 1–880463–09–1

Library of Congress Catalog Card Number: 97-092421

Rising Sun Publishing, Inc.
P.O. Box 70906
Marietta, Georgia 30007-0906
(800) 524-2813
email:info@rspublishing.com
visit web site at http://www.rspublishing.com

Printed in the United States of America.

Dedication

This book is dedicated to my wife Nina who has stood by me
in all that God has led us through.

Let thy fountains be blessed: and rejoice with the
wife of thy youth.

[Proverbs 5:18]

Acknowledgements

I would like to give praise and thanks to God who guided
our steps into the anointed ministry of our former pastor
Dr. Frederick K.C. Price, III of Crenshaw Christian Center in
Los Angeles, California, and into the anointed ministry of our
current pastor, Cleflo A. Dollar of World Changers Ministries in
College Park, Georgia.

I would like to thank Dr. Pamela Powell, Patrice Kincey, Janice
Allen, Pat Lachelt, and the teachers of the Pasadena Unified
School District who prayed, helped, or otherwise played a
role in my getting the medical care that saved my life.

I would like to thank the team of Cardiologists, Orthopedic
Surgeons, Infectious Disease Specialists, Kidney Specialists,
Neurologists, and Blood Specialist led by the special
anointing of Dr. Nathan Lewis.

I would like to thank the nurses, orderlies, lab technicians, and
others at the St. Luke Medical Center in Pasadena, California,
who in their own special ways helped me through it all.

Finally, I would like to thank my editor, Denise Mitchell Smith of
Covina, California; Juanita Clark for her gift of prophesy; my
friends and family; the many prayer partners; and those interceding,
who prayed healing prayers daily on my behalf.

Contents

About the Author

Commit thy works unto the Lord, and thy thoughts shall be established.

[Proverbs 16:3]

Mychal Wynn has often been described as one of God's "Triple A Warriors:" Anointed, Appointed, and Approved! He is the author of several books and regularly speaks to parents, teachers, and children throughout the United States. God has anointed him with the unique ability to integrate educational research, hands-on experiences, and a long-term vision, into easily understood and easily implementable strategies and techniques for turning schools into places of passion and purpose for our children. While God's Word clearly outlines "What" the responsibilities of parents and teachers are in raising and teaching children, Mychal's writing and workshops outline "How" to do it.

> *But the Lord said unto me, Say not, I am a child: for thou shalt go to all that I shall send thee, and whatsoever I command thee thou shalt speak. Be not afraid of their faces: for I am with thee to deliver thee, saith the Lord. Then the Lord put forth His hand, and touched my mouth. And the Lord said unto me, Behold, I have put my words in thy mouth.*
>
> [Jeremiah 1:7-9]

Mychal, his wife, Nina, and their sons Mychal-David, and Jalani live in Marietta, Georgia.

Foreword

*My heart is inditing a good matter: I speak of
the things which I have made touching the
King: my tongue is the pen of a ready writer.*
[Psalm 45:1]

I was three days into my hospital stay when, in one of my
conversations with God, He told me to share my testimony
of this experience through the means that He had anointed
me, which were to write and to speak. While some who read
this book may not share my faith and my personal beliefs, they
will appreciate the testimony of how my faith took me
through a difficult, life-threatening, situation. There was no
doubt in the minds of my doctors that I was near death and
that while they did everything within their knowledge to
combat the infection that sent my body into septic shock, they
could only watch and witness my healing.

This book began as a testimony of my hospital experience.
However, through Divine Inspiration, it has become much more.
As I began to write this book, I realized that my testimony didn't
begin in the hospital but at birth. As I reflected on my own life
I realized that for each of us, what we do is guided by our
experiences and what we believe. Our experiences could be
considered the lessons of life: our education, our relationships,
our successes, and our failures. Our beliefs reflect our faith,
our perspectives, and our attitudes about ourselves and others.
While it could be argued that our experiences shape our beliefs,
I believe that it is our beliefs that shape our experiences.

For example, when I begin a task, I believe I can complete it. When I begin a competition, I believe I can win it. When I encounter a problem, I believe I can resolve it. While I do not believe that I am all powerful, all knowing or even always capable, I have faith that God is! This faith shapes my attitude. My attitude or beliefs, cause me to enter the race with all odds against me. If I am in the race, there always exists the opportunity of winning-no matter how improbable. When I begin a task, no matter how great the challenges or how difficult the obstacles, there is always a chance-no matter how slim-that I can successfully complete the task. Thus, because of what I believe, my faith, I choose to engage in endeavors that shape my experiences. In fact, because of my faith, I undertook the task of writing this book through which I will share my testimony. In another regard, my work, education, successes, failures, etc., combined with my pre-existing beliefs shaped what I did during my hospitalization. They shaped my relationships with the doctors, nurses, and hospital staff. They shaped my attitude toward the days and nights of confinement to a bed, barely able to move. They shaped my attitude toward the humiliating experiences of the Foley catheter, bed pan, and the inability to bathe myself.

This book has become more than a recalling of my hospital experiences, it has become a testimony of the power of the human spirit; a testimony of the healing power of the Holy Spirit; a testimony of the power of the love and prayers of people interceding for my well-being; and ultimately a personal testimony of my relationship with God, my belief in His anointing, and my trust in His power, grace, and mercy.

The words of a man's mouth are as deep waters,
and the wellspring of wisdom as a flowing brook.
[Proverbs 18:4]

– Mychal Wynn

INTRODUCTION

We All Have a Story to Tell

*He gave some, apostles: and some, prophets;
and some, evangelists; and some, pastors and
teachers; For the perfecting of the saints, for the
work of the ministry, for the edifying of the
body of Christ.*

[Ephesians 4:11,12]

This book is my testimony to God's grace, mercy, and omnipotent power. I have heard many testimonies of how God's grace and mercy have enabled others to overcome drugs, alcohol abuse, or otherwise broken and defeated lives. While sharing in the joy of their deliverance, I could never personally identify with the obstacles that they had to overcome. Long before I was "born again," I believed in the adage: "Your attitude determines your altitude." Through the Word of God, I would later learn that Jesus said: "Your faith has made you whole." What the world calls a "positive attitude" God calls "faith." Those with a positive attitude believe in a positive outcome even when one is not guaranteed. Those who have faith believe through the power of God that all things are possible.

Faith is the substance of things hoped for, the evidence of things not seen.
[Hebrews 11:1]

I have never been addicted to drugs or alcohol. I have never questioned God's omnipotent power or Satan's destructive potential. In fact, while Satan has formed many weapons against me, I have stood faithfully according to God's Word, as one having power and authority over the works of the Devil.

Behold, I give unto you power to tread on serpents and scorpions, and over all the power of the enemy: and nothing shall by any means hurt you.
[Luke 10:19]

By most measures, my life has been a testimony of victory. Born in a one room shack in Pike County, Alabama, an under-nourished, unattractive, little baby, I was barely six months old when I was given up for adoption. I was taken in by parents whose prayers protected me from the dangers and despair of growing up in Chicago's south side urban ghetto: an area of broken spirits and shattered dreams, a place where desperation and despair claims the lives of young and old each day. I saw friends and relatives trapped by their own negative thinking despite talents and abilities that could have enabled them to enjoy the richness and abundance of God's creation. By and large they were defeated as they lacked the vision to see the tremendous potential and possibilities for their lives.

Where there is no vision, the people perish...
[Proverbs 29:18]

Many of my friends and relatives didn't lack talents and abilities whether athletic or analytical, verbal or visual. In fact, many of them had talents and abilities that I was in awe of. I was, perhaps, among the least talented. I couldn't draw. I couldn't run. I stammered as a child, so Lord knows that I couldn't talk.

> *And Moses said unto the Lord, O my Lord, I*
> *am not eloquent, neither heretofore, nor since*
> *thou hast spoken unto thy servant: but I am*
> *slow of speech, and of a slow tongue.*
>
> [Exodus 4:10]

I grew up in a community that celebrated athletes, that envied those who could play "The Dozens," that admired those who displayed their artistic talents through graffiti, that feared those who could fight and loved those who were beautiful. While those around me got all of the attention through running, jumping, talking, drawing, fighting or looking good, I learned early that the Lord had anointed me with the simple and little-appreciated ability to write. Only later in life would I understand how God anoints each person differently: that the anointing of the athlete is no less than the anointing of the scholar, that the anointing of the artist is no less than the anointing of the physician, that the anointing of the carpenter is no less than the anointing of the teacher.

> *Now there are diversities of gifts, but the same*
> *Spirit... For one is given by the Spirit the word*
> *of wisdom; to another, the word of knowledge*
> *by the same Spirit; to another, faith by the same*
> *Spirit; to another, the gifts of healing by the*
> *same Spirit; to another, the working of miracles;*

to another, prophecy; to another discerning of
spirits; to another, divers kinds of tongues; to
another, the interpretation of tongues: But all
these worketh that one and the self-same Spirit,
dividing to every man severally "as He will."
[1 Corinthians 12:4,8-11]

I'm not sure whether the anointing that came upon me was predetermined or whether God anointed me based on the desires of my heart.

Before I formed thee in the belly, I knew thee;
and before thou camest forth out of the womb I
sanctified thee...
[Jeremiah 1:5]

I began developing a love for writing in the second grade while attending Edmund Burke Elementary School. I would challenge my classmates to name anything and I would write a verse about it–whether it be a pencil, a pig, a truck, or a fly. You name it and I could write a verse about it.

There was a fly, who buzzed in my ear
He flew so fast, he had nothing to fear.
I waived my hand to shoo him away
But he kept on buzzing, determined to stay.
I grabbed a book, and took a swing
I missed the fly, but I hit something.
My mother's lamp fell to the floor
And at that very moment I heard a key in the door.
Mama is home, but how can I explain
That the buzzing of a fly had driven me insane?
So I grabbed the lamp and put it back in place
While the fly kept buzzing, with a smile on his face!

If this was, in fact, my predestined anointing, God must have been disappointed that my schooling did more to hinder rather than to develop my talents and desires. Despite the fact that writing was my passion, I never found a teacher, preacher or counselor who encouraged me to lay hold of my passion and pursue developing my talent. Because of my high test scores and grades in math and science, I was encouraged to pursue a career in engineering. Not knowing any better, I abandoned my "childish" dream. After graduating high school, I attended college to pursue a degree in electrical engineering. Despite my abilities, I never developed the same passion for calculus and physics as I did for poetry and prose. While a degree in electrical engineering could guarantee a job—not to mention a higher salary—than a degree in English, literature, or journalism, engineering wasn't my passion. Becoming an engineer was not fulfillment of my anointing.

Without counsel and advice about how to pursue my dream or how to bring the full anointing of God upon me, I went on to attend Northeastern University in Boston, Massachusetts, majoring, first, in electrical engineering; and later, in business and computer science. After graduating with honors, with a degree in business and computer science, I discovered that there were many well-paying jobs awaiting me. I eventually accepted a job offer from IBM in San Jose, California. After two years of trying to fit in; trying to confirm to a rigid corporate environment; trying to understand, let alone accept, office politics, I left a high-paying job to follow my dream of becoming a writer. Little, by way of my academic or professional development, prepared me for this. I knew little to nothing about becoming a writer. I knew absolutely nothing about the publishing business. This was to become the first of many tests of my faith. I would later learn that this leap of faith, while a babe in Christ, would lead me into the full anointing of God and into the abundance of His Kingdom.

For we walk by faith, not by sight...
[2 Corinthians 5:7]

Leaving IBM to pursue writing and selling poetry on t-shirts and posters along the boardwalk of Venice Beach, California, I went from making nearly $50,000 dollars a year to making just a few hundred dollars each weekend. Many were quick to point out the foolishness of my leaving the comfort and security of a well-paying job to pursue the uncertain future of a dream. Yet, with limited knowledge and dwindling financial resources, my unwavering faith was reaffirmed and ultimately rewarded. A good friend, mentor, and anointed woman of God, Dr. Terre Finley, a former classroom teacher and now a program director in the Los Angeles School District, prophesied that the gates of Heaven would be opened up unto me and that the riches of the Kingdom would flow upon me, that I had found favor with God, and that I needed simply to maintain my faith. God was preparing me with a special anointing that would some day be revealed to me.

He that prophesieth speaketh unto men to edification, and exhortation, and comfort.
[1 Corinthians 14:3]

As Dr. Finley had prophesied, over the years, God anointed my writing. Although writing was my dream, I have learned that God blesses us, not for ourselves but for the benefit of others. While my early ambition was to write poetry, God anointed me to write books and materials that would bless parents, teachers, and the children whom we are responsible for parenting and teaching. Despite having once had a severe stammering problem, God anointed me to breathe life into the words that I had written as the power of the Holy Spirit enabled me to motivate, challenge, and inspire parents and their children in schools, churches, community organizations, and at national conferences throughout the United States, Canada, and in the Caribbean. Fulfilling the desires of our hearts, my wife and I were blessed with a trip to the African countries of Egypt and Ghana. We journeyed up the Nile River and across the continent to the slave dungeons on the West Coast where our ancestors began their journey across the Atlantic. Humbled by the experience Nina and I left the continent of Africa with revelation knowledge all in preparation for the work that God was preparing us to do and for the challenges that Satan would bring against us.

But the Comforter, which is the Holy Ghost, whom the Father will send in my name, He shall teach you all things, and bring all things to your remembrance, whatsoever I have said unto you.
[John 14:26]

In the ten years that we have been married, my wife and I have persevered through each burden and obstacle that we have encountered. We have forged through each test to discover God's blessings awaiting us on the other side. We have witnessed the birth of two extraordinarily handsome and intelligent sons after doctors told my wife that she couldn't bear children. We have witnessed my writing and our publishing business go from a part-time endeavor to a full-time blessing.

> *Blessed is every one that feareth the Lord; that walketh in His ways. For thou shalt eat the labour of thine hands: Happy shalt thou be, and it shall be well with thee. Thy wife shall be as a fruitful vine by the sides of thine house: thy children like olive-plants round about thy table.*
> [Psalm 128:1-3]

While working together has its challenges and pitfalls, my wife and I have been blessed with the joy and freedom that working together affords us. Not only have I been blessed to spend quality time with her, my best friend, but I have quality time to share with our eight-year-old son, my best pal and our three-year-old son with his limitless energy.

From the undernourished, unattractive, abandoned little baby to a mother and father who loved and guided me; from the loneliness of a childhood in which I never seemed to fit in to a wife and children who surround me each day with love; from the shotgun shack where I was born to a 5500 square foot home in Marietta, Georgia; from the poverty and hand-me-down clothes of my childhood to the Versace, Zegna, Calvin Klein, Donna Karan, Armani, and Brioni suits in my closet and the Mercedes and Suburban parked in the garage, God has truly opened up the gates of Heaven and poured abundant blessings upon us.

Walking in God's grace, Nina and I overcame each burden and broke each yoke that challenged us. In marriage, in parenting, in finances, and in dealing with the emotional baggage carried around since our childhoods, we had claimed victory through the Word of God. With me as the cornerstone of our family, my writing and speaking being the primary sources of income, we faced yet another challenge. One day I stood in the best physical condition of my life. The next, I was near death. Totally unexpected and without forewarning, my case baffled doctors and provided a proving ground for what I believed. There were no other ways for Satan to attack me: my faith, unwavering; my anointing, affirmed; my wife and I standing upon the Word of God for our strength and our salvation.

This book tells the story of how God's grace and mercy brought me through my infirmities and revealed to me a fuller purpose in my life. And, how my unwavering spirit and faith sustained me through it all.

> ...*I have heard thy prayers, I have seen thy tears:*
> *behold, I will heal thee...*
>
> [2 Kings 20:5]

For therein is the righteousness of God revealed from faith to faith: as it is written, The just shall live by faith.

[Romans 1:17]

CHAPTER I

A Testimony to God's Grace and Mercy

I will speak of thy testimonies also before kings,
and will not be ashamed.
[Psalm 119:46]

Wednesday, March 19, 1997, began as a normal day. My wife and I got our two sons off to school, did our weight-training workout, and worked together in our business. On this day, I was scheduled to fly to Los Angeles. I would be speaking to over eight hundred teachers in Pasadena, California, at a conference on Thursday and to the combined teaching staffs from several schools on Friday. I would spend Saturday with friends and family in Los Angeles and return to Atlanta on Sunday.

My speaking and training schedule requires that I travel to school districts, colleges, national conferences, and appear before various organizations throughout the country. In the fifteen years that I have been speaking, I have been blessed to have never missed a speaking engagement. God has placed a hedge around me like Job, protecting me in my travels despite delayed or cancelled flights, missed connections or other events beyond my control.

Hast not Thou made a hedge about him, and
about his house, and about all that he hath on
every side? Thou hast blessed the work of his
hands, and his substance is increased in the land.
                                         Job [1:10]

This routine trip to Los Angeles would prove to be anything but routine. Less than twenty-four hours after arriving in Los Angeles, I spent the next twenty-seven days hospitalized at the St. Luke Medical Center in Pasadena, California, in a case that baffled a team of fifteen doctors. I entered the hospital for twenty-four hours observation with what I thought was a bruised arm. By the time I was released, twenty-seven days later, my faith had withstood the test of unexpected and unexplained infirmities that took me to the brink of death. How precarious our position is in life!

Each time that the Devil has raised his ugly head against our family, God's grace and mercy has sustained us. Despite all of our material possessions and business success, Satan pushed my wife and me to the brink of divorce. Yet, God's grace led us to Reverend and Mrs. Canty at the New Birth Missionary Baptist Church, who counseled and guided us back into a wholesome, healthy, God-centered marriage. Our oldest son was constantly challenged with a violent temper and disrespectful behavior at school that left him unhappy and left us confused. Like Dr. Jekyll and Mr. Hyde, our son was perfect and upright at home and a terror at school. Hardly a week went by that we weren't being called to his school to meet with teachers or the principal regarding yet another fight, pushing, or other incident. His first grade field day was typical. All of

the children were participating in outdoor track and
activities. Mychal-David became upset with another little b
who tried to cut into the line, so he grabbed and choked the
little boy right there in front of the parents, teachers,
principal, and all of the other children.

Again, God's grace and mercy helped us to help him sow
good seeds which eventually resulted in a significant change
in his behavior. As our son's personal attitude changed, his
academic success soared. His high standardized test scores
qualified him for the Talented and Gifted program. God
further anointed him with extraordinary artistic talents and
verbal skills that have found favor for him among both children
and adults. Indeed, we have witnessed much for the Lord!

> *Keep therefore and do them; for this is your*
> *wisdom and your understanding in the sight of*
> *the nations, which shall hear all these statutes,*
> *and say, Surely this great nation is a wise and*
> *understanding people. For what nation is there*
> *so great, who hath God so nigh unto them, as*
> *the Lord our God is in all things that we call*
> *upon him for?*
>
> [Deuteronomy 4:6,7]

CHAPTER 2

This is the Day that the Lord has Made

This is the day that the Lord has made; we will rejoice and be glad in it.

[Psalm 118:24]

I set the alarm for 5:45 A.M., but as usual, I awoke before the alarm went off. I was anxious about today. I was looking forward–not only to my normal workout routine–but to leaving town for my first major speaking engagement of the year. This speaking engagement would be the first of several over the coming weeks. I was scheduled to speak at schools, churches, and conferences in Austin, Texas; Columbia, South Carolina; Hartford, Connecticut; Akron, Cleveland, and Columbus, Ohio; Chapel Hill, North Carolina; and at the University of Maryland.

Each book that I have written and each speech that I've given have been divinely-inspired opportunities for sowing good seeds. This first trip of the year to the Pasadena school district would be another such opportunity. By allowing God's anointing to work within me and to speak through me, the teachers, principals, and school board members in attendance would benefit in expanding their knowledge, strategies, and understanding on behalf of children. As a result all would be blessed, thus, good seeds would be sown. I love what I do, I get paid to do it, and it results in a blessing for a lot of people!

> *And it shall come to pass in that day, that his*
> *burden shall be taken away from off thy*
> *shoulder, and his yoke from off thy neck, and the*
> *yoke shall be destroyed because of the anointing.*
> [Isaiah 10:27]

I climbed out of bed and put on my running shorts, t-shirt, socks, and sneakers. My wife Nina, our two sons, Mychal-David and Jalani, and Poky, our dog, were all still asleep. I climbed into my car to drive over to the gym for my morning run on the treadmill. Later that morning I would join Nina for our weight workout. Not only was I intent on being a mighty warrior before the Lord with the words of my mouth and the stroke of my pen, but I wanted my body, a temple of the living God, to have the look of power and authority as I testified to the grace, mercy, and omnipotent power of God.

> *What! know ye not that your body is the temple*
> *of the Holy Ghost which is in you, which you*
> *have of God, and ye are not your own?*
> [1 Corinthians 6:19]

While I have always worked to keep myself in good overall physical condition, it was Nina who got me into weight training. Nina had a personal goal to compete and win a body building competition. She was intrigued by the prospects of shaping her 40-plus year-old body into 118 pounds of lean muscle, allowing her to compete against much younger women. Achieving that weight would be nearly a 25 pound weight loss and would require maintaining a strick dietary discipline and a workout routine. Nina was excited at the power of such a testimony to those who struggle with obesity, lack of exercise, or other destructive devices that shorten their lives as they destroy the temples of God. Her attitude and her testimony was, "If I can do it, so can you!"

During today's workout, I was doing a movement called "front arm rows." On the last set of the routine, I got carried away watching my shoulder definition in the mirror and I banged the weights against the underside of my left elbow. "Ouch!" It caused a sore from a previous spider bite on my elbow to reopen and to bleed slightly. I put the weights down and washed the blood off. Fadi, a young body builder from Lebanon was training me. He put a band-aid on my elbow. I continued my workout.

Finishing about noon, Nina and I went to the market for groceries. It felt good to "strut" with my wife around the grocery store, muscles defined and bulging. I was so proud of Nina: looking good, following her dream, being my partner, a dedicated mother, and a continuing testimony of faith, courage, and determination.

> *How fair is thy love, my sister, my spouse!*
> *How much better is thy love than wine! and*
> *the smell of thine ointments than all spices!*
> *Thy lips, Oh my spouse, drop as the honeycomb:*
> *honey and milk are under thy tongue; and*
> *the smell of thy garments is like the smell*
> *of Lebanon.*
> [Songs of Solomon 4:10,11]

I can still remember how most of her friends, and even some of her family told her that she was crazy to believe in me and my dreams. There's a saying that is repeated frequently in the church: "God will make a way out of no way." I guess they didn't think that it applied to Nina and me. Throughout my life, I have learned that when people tell you that it can't be done, they usually have to get out of the way of someone who is doing it!

After we returned home, I left Nina to go and get my hair cut. I returned later and showered, finished packing, and got dressed. The Lord knows that I was looking good and lean. Now don't get me wrong there was no vanity, no ego, only confidence in the power and authority promised by God and received through Christ. After all Jesus told us, "Let your light shine."

> *Let your light so shine before men, that they*
> *may see your good works, and glorify your*
> *Father which is in heaven.*
>
> [Matthew 5:16]

My Versace shirt and Brioni suit, clean cut and confident walk, were all testimonies to God's omnipotent power; all done to His glory; all providing testimony of His grace and mercy. When people of the world look good, are financially successful, and are admired by others, they draw people to the things of the world. Likewise, when people of God look good, are financially successful, have healthy and wholesome relationships, and speak with confidence and self-assurance, through their example and their testimony, they draw people unto God and into His church.

I often talk to young men and women who have strayed away from the church. I am able to provide a living testimony to the mercy, grace, compassion, and omnipotent power of God. After seeing and hearing me, they come and ask questions. They want to know how to put the Word of God into action in their lives. Our conversations draw many of them back to God. Thus, I let my light shine to the glory of God!

I was only planning to be gone for three days and I normally would drive myself to the airport. I don't like to burden Nina with having to drive through traffic and rearranging her schedule or disrupting the normal routine for our two sons. Today however, I was led to have Nina drive me to the airport. I had scheduled my return for Sunday morning, allowing enough time for Nina to pick me up and continue to church. Upon arriving at the airport, I hugged and said good-bye to Nina, Mychal-David, and Jalani and went to my gate to board a Delta Airlines flight to Los Angeles. I settled into a comfortable first-class seat where I did some reading and made notes for my presentation the next day.

> *The spirit of the Lord God is upon me; because the Lord hath anointed me to preach good tidings unto the meek; He hath sent me to bind up the brokenhearted, to proclaim liberty to the captives, and the opening of the prison to them that are bound.*
>
> [Isaiah 61:1]

Chapter 3

No Weapon Formed Against Me

We are troubled on every side, yet not distressed;
perplexed, but not in despair; persecuted, but
not forsaken; cast down, but not destroyed.
[2 Corinthians 4:8,9]

When the plane landed in Los Angeles, my left elbow felt a little stiff. But this was to be expected considering that I bumped it pretty hard during my workout. I flexed my arm several times to relieve the stiffness as I walked to baggage claim. I retrieved my suitcase, two boxes of books, and boarded the Hertz bus to pick up my rental car. Once at the rental car lot, I carried my suitcase and boxes of books to the car with no problem.

I drove off of the rental car lot and stopped at a grocery store to pick up the things that I needed to maintain my diet over the next three days. In addition to maintaining my diet, I was planning to run two to three miles each morning and meet my sister-in-law, Becky, at the health club on Saturday.

After I got my groceries, I made the twenty-minute drive from the airport to my friends' home, Wayne and Jacqui Miller, in Carson, California. By the time I got to their home, there was more swelling in my arm although I still didn't have much pain. I got to their home about 11:15 P.M. Wayne and I talked for a while. After Wayne went to bed, I ironed my clothes for the next day. My arm stiffened more and began to throb. As I laid down about 1:30 A.M. the pain was more than I could bear. I didn't want to wake Wayne and Jacqui so I looked through the medicine cabinet and found some Tylenol. I lay down across the bed and placed my arm on a bag of ice.

Oh, God, does it hurt! I lay there unable to sleep, thinking about my presentation when I heard Wayne get up. I looked over at the clock and it was already 4:30 A.M. By this time, my arm was completely swollen and had limited mobility. I asked Wayne to help me make a sling. We tried one of his wife's scarves, but that wasn't long enough. So Wayne loaned me a belt.

With my make-shift sling, I got up and went downstairs to load 12 boxes of books into my car. In addition to the 2 boxes that I had brought with me, we had shipped 10 boxes to their home. With Wayne's help, I got all of the boxes loaded into the car. I tried to eat breakfast, but between the pain in my arm and my fever, I lost my appetite. I grabbed a cup of coffee and went upstairs to shower and dress.

Forgetting the pain in my arm, my adrenaline was pumping as I mentally prepared myself to speak later that morning. This was my work; my special anointing. I was planning to present three workshops based on the material covered in two of my books. My shower went well and, surprisingly, I managed to comb my hair with only one hand. Wayne had gone for his morning walk so I asked his wife, Jacqui, to help me button the top button of my shirt and to help me with my necktie.

I was anxious to get started on the thirty-minute drive from Carson to Pasadena. If I could get on the road by 6:00 A.M., I felt that I could get through Los Angeles before rush-hour traffic. Not withstanding the sling, I was still intent on looking good for my presentation. I was wearing a navy blue three button Italian suit, custom fitted white shirt, and a white and yellow Versace tie.

It took Jacqui nearly twenty minutes to button the top button of my shirt. She was afraid of pinching my neck, so she had a time trying to get the shirt buttoned. I was of no help. I couldn't lift my left arm any higher than my stomach. Finally, Jacqui affirmed, "Holy Father, send the Holy Spirit to us to button this button so that Mychal may go and do your work." In the next moment, "Touchdown!"

> *Let us therefore come boldly unto the throne of grace, that we may obtain mercy, and find grace to help in time of need.*
> [Hebrews 4:16]

Despite the fact that my arm was in excruciating pain, I had no intention of calling Nina. Whenever I left town, Nina's hands were full with Mychal-David, Jalani, managing our household, and the demands of our business. I certainly didn't want to burden her with another worry. I climbed into my rental car about 6:15 A.M., sling and all, and hit the freeways that would take me north through Los Angeles into Pasadena. I praised God that the traffic wasn't bad and trusted God that the ride wouldn't take long. People must have thought that I had lost my mind as I drove along the freeway rocking back and forth in pain, unable to find a comfortable position. My arm was hurting so badly that I turned up the music and began singing to take my mind off of the pain.

I will sing unto the Lord as long as I live: I will sing praise to my God while I have my being.
[Psalm 104:33]

Through the grace of God, I pulled into the Elliot Middle School parking lot about 7:00 A.M. Dr. Pamela Powell, the Director of Elementary Instruction for the Pasadena School District, met me in the parking lot. I told her how I had bruised my arm working out with weights the previous day and reassured her that while it hurt, it wouldn't hinder me from presenting my message to the teachers. Dr. Powell kindly had the custodian unload my boxes and she, together with some of her staff, had all of the books unpacked and organized on tables in the auditorium where I was scheduled to give my presentation. Since I was in no condition to concern myself with speaking and handling book sales, Dr. Powell called upon Patrice Kincey, a first grade teacher, to handle the sale of my books and materials.

Patrice was full of energy with an attention to detail. She wanted to know the price of each book, whether or not I collected Sales Tax, if teachers could write checks, who the checks should be made payable to, if I had a receipt book, and so on. While Patrice was asking me questions, I stood there running a fever, my arm swollen, and in pain. I just nodded my head. I finally said, "I trust you to figure it out. Whatever you decide will be okay." Patrice stood there with the most beautiful smile, so tiny that her first grade students didn't have to strain their necks to look up to her. Patrice nodded her head and said, "Don't worry I'll take care of it." Patrice would prove to be one of God's ministering angels as she went from selling my books to saving my life!

> He shall give His angels charge over thee, to
> keep thee in all thy ways.
>
> [Psalm 91:11]

After turning all of my books and materials over to Patrice, Dr. Powell called Pat Lachelt, the Superintendent of Nursing, to come over to look at my arm. Pat graciously made a real sling and an ice pack for me. I would later learn that she had confided in Dr. Powell some real concerns. "Pam, Mychal's arm is burning up and swollen twice it's normal size. The sling and the ice pack will help, but we had better get him to a doctor when this is over." Pat kept an eye on me throughout the morning. Nearing the end of the morning, she confided to Dr. Powell that she was concerned that the swelling in my arm was intensifying and that it was hot to the touch. She feared that if they didn't get me to a doctor soon, my condition would worsen to the point that I could lose my arm! Little did she know that in the next twenty-four hours, not only was I on the verge of losing my arm, but that I would stand at the doorway of death as my body went into septic shock!

Despite Pat's concerns, I was pumped up to talk to the teachers in attendance. I forgot all about the swelling and the pain in my arm. At 8:15 A.M., I began the first of three presentations. I shared with teachers my good news/bad news testimony. The bad news was that I would be wearing a sling preventing me from being as animated as I normally would be; but the good news was that in the entire fifteen years that I had been travelling and speaking, through God's grace and mercy, I had never missed a speaking engagement. Today would be no exception.

Following the first presentation, many teachers came forward to purchase books. A good friend of mine, Janice Allen, an elementary school principal, who was instrumental in my being there, came up to see how I was doing. Unconvinced that I was doing okay, despite my assurances that my arm "hurts just a little," she kept a watchful eye on me throughout the day. As I sat on the stage, teachers brought their books to me to autograph. I eagerly talked with teachers and signed their books. At the beginning of the second presentation, with God's anointing fully upon me, I took my arm out of the sling becoming animated as I waived my arms in my enthusiasm. I felt so good that I left the stage during the presentation and walked throughout the audience to interact and answer questions. Following the second presentation, the pain returned, causing me to put my arm back into the sling. Although I still had a lot of energy, I could feel myself weakening. At the end of my final presentation, I asked the audience if I could sit down. I was totally exhausted.

> *Have mercy upon me, O Lord; for I am weak:*
> *O Lord, heal me; for my bones are vexed.*
> [Psalm 6:2]

One teacher approached me and asked, "Mr. Wynn, is the swollen arm the one that you sign with?" She was so happy when I mumbled, "No, the hand that I sign with is okay." She and the other teachers held their books open while I used my good arm to sign them. Finally, Dr. Powell asked everyone to leave me alone. Patrice had called hers and Dr. Powell's personal physician, Dr. Nathan Lewis, who agreed to see me. Patrice was planning to drive me to Dr. Lewis' office not far from the school. Now that my presentations were over, I began to relax, I was mentally and physically drained. As I got into Patrice's car she noticed as I leaned back into the seat and closed my eyes. She shared with me later that she was afraid that I might die on the way to Dr. Lewis' office!

> *For indeed he was sick near unto death: but*
> *God had mercy on him.*
>
> [Philippians 2:27]

CHAPTER 4

Let Me Get on with the Work that God has Called Me To Do

Be anxious for nothing; but in all things through prayer and supplication with thanksgiving let your requests be made known unto God.
[Philippians 4:6]

After arriving at Dr. Lewis' office I explained the events of the day before. Dr. Lewis believed that the swelling was related to the accident with the weights. After an initial examination, he ordered an x-ray. I was so tired that I almost fell asleep waiting for the x-ray technician. The x-ray didn't reveal a stress fracture so Dr. Lewis did some probing and took some fluid from my elbow to test for an infection.

While Dr. Lewis was examining my arm, I was concerned about getting home so that I could rest in preparation for my presentations the next day. Then, it occurred to me how much this medical examination might cost me, so in my mind, I began going over alternative forms of payment for his bill. I thought that perhaps he might simply prescribe some medication for my arm and I could give him a few books in trade. I had never been in a hospital. I had never been sick other than an occasional cold. I hadn't seen a doctor since my examination for a life insurance policy two years before. Although I had medical insurance, I had never used it. It never occurred to me that my medical insurance would pay for Dr. Lewis' examination. Totally unaware of the seriousness of my condition I was already thinking beyond my physical condition, to my financial condition and what Dr. Lewis' examination was going to cost me.

With all of this going through my mind, I asked, "Dr. Lewis, how much is this examination going to cost me? How about some books in trade?" While I was talking, Dr. Lewis continued examining me and apparently ignoring me. At the conclusion of his examination, he asked that if he prescribed an oral antibiotic would I go straight home and rest? "Yes, sir, Dr. Lewis. You don't have to worry about me. I will be glad to go home and get some rest!" I thought to myself, "Yes, I can get a few pills, go home, catch some Zs, and tomorrow I can get on with the program!"

I don't know if Dr. Lewis knew what I was thinking, but he just smiled and said, "We're going to check you into the hospital overnight. Once there, we can give you some intravenous antibiotics and re-evaluate your arm in the morning."

"But Dr. Lewis, will I be able to be released from the hospital in time to make my presentations? Patrice, what time are my presentations scheduled for tomorrow?" Everyone just smiled. No one appeared to be paying any attention to me!

Dr. Lewis made arrangements for me to be admitted to the St. Luke Medical Center in Pasadena. Earlier, Dr. Powell had made arrangements to have my remaining books and materials packed and my rental car returned. We left Dr. Lewis' office and Patrice and Pat drove me to the hospital. As we got into Patrice's car, my attention refocused on my arm which was now nearly as big as my leg.

> *Blessed be the God of Shadrach, Meshach, and*
> *Abednego, who hath sent His angel, and*
> *delivered His servants that trusted in Him.*
> *[Daniel 3:28]*

When we got to the hospital, Pat went inside to arrange for a wheelchair and I climbed aboard. Praise God, there wasn't a line, because it seemed like an eternity while they took my medical insurance card and had me sign admittance forms. I was almost unconscious. I slumped over in the wheelchair. The pain was killing me. My temperature was 103 degrees. My throat was dry and my arm was burning up. I needed some water. "Please, get me some water."

By the time they got me into a room, it was nearly 5:00 P.M. I had been awake nearly thirty-six hours. I was dead tired. My arm felt like someone was beating it with a sledge hammer and now looked like an elephant leg. "Jesus help me. I still have to get up and speak to the teachers tomorrow! If I don't speak I don't get paid."

> *But if any provide not for his own, and*
> *specially for those of his own house, he hath*
> *denied the faith, and is worse than an infidel.*
> *[1 Timothy 5:8]*

I've never missed a speaking engagement and I don't intend to allow a swollen arm to keep me from doing the work that the Lord has anointed me to do. There was so much going through my mind that I didn't realize that the nurse was putting me into the bed.

The nurse got me out of my clothes and into a hospital gown (you know the one that flaps in the back so that everyone can see your butt). I entrusted my clothes and jewelry to Patrice. I had met Patrice for the first time today. I didn't even know her last name. Not to worry, Patrice was undoubtedly one of God's "Triple A Women:" Anointed, Appointed, and Approved. Like a ministering angel, she had seen me through the day; taken charge over my books, materials, and $2,000 in money earned from the book sales following my presentations at the school. She had begun the healing process and possibly saved my life by making the appointment with her own personal physician, another of God's anointed. She had taken me to the doctor and finally to the hospital.

> *The angel of the Lord encampeth round about*
> *them that fear him, and delivereth them. O*
> *taste and see that the Lord is good: blessed is the*
> *man that trusteth in Him.*
> [Psalm 34:7,8]

As I lay back onto the bed, the nurse finally gave me something for the pain, a shot of Demerol. As I closed my eyes, the nurse took my right arm and inserted two intravenous lines. I didn't pay any attention to the needles as the pain was finally subsiding. The nurse connected an antibiotic solution and fluids to the I.V.s and put two pillows under my left arm to keep it elevated above my heart. My arm not only looked like an elephant's leg, but was so heavy that felt like an elephant's leg.

Being assured that I was in good hands, Patrice and Pat said good-bye. Patrice told me that she would take my things home with her and that she would be checking on me the next day. I lay there looking up at the ceiling with the two I.V.s in my right arm and at my left arm setting on top of the two pillows and thought, "Oh what a day, what a day, what a day."

> *Therefore I take pleasure in infirmities, in reproaches, in necessities, in persecutions, in distresses for Christ's sake; for when I am weak, then am I strong.*
> [2 Corinthians 12:10]

CHAPTER 5

Demerol Demons

Thou scarest me with dreams, and terrifiest me through visions.

[Job 7:14]

Having resolved that I was really in the hospital, I decided to call Nina. The telephone rang and the answering machine clicked on. I was glad that Nina wasn't there since I didn't know exactly what to say. I wasn't concerned about myself as much as I was about her. I didn't want her to worry; it was all in God's hands. As I began the message, I said:

> *"Hi Honey. I have some good news and some bad news. The good news is that I did a great job today with the teachers. The evaluations were outstanding and they really seemed to understand the message that I shared with them. They bought a lot of books. Some of the school board members were there and it looks like they will be having me back again."*

My voice began to tremble:

> *"Well, the bad news is that I'm in the hospital. It appears that my arm was injured more seriously than we thought. Everything is okay, but I saw a doctor today and he wants to keep*

me in the hospital overnight for observation.
The number here at the hospital is... Don't
worry about me, Honey, I love you."

After leaving the message for Nina, I called Wayne to let him and Jacqui know that I wouldn't be coming back tonight. Jacqui answered the telephone and I mumbled that I was in the hospital. I don't know what else I said because the Demerol caused me to drift off to sleep. About an hour later, I was awakened by the telephone. It was Nina. She asked what had happened and I mumbled something about my arm being swollen as a result of my workout the day before. I went on to say that I had a shot that was making me sleepy and that she shouldn't worry. I would call her back first thing in the morning. Besides, they were only going to keep me for twenty-four hours.

After talking to Nina, I drifted back to sleep. I had a dream where someone was chasing me. There were bright colors all around and a bright light in my face. I had come to the edge of a cliff and was about to lose my balance when I was awakened by a nurse. It was around midnight. I had a fever and my arm was throbbing. "I need to take your temperature and blood pressure, Mychal." I looked up at her and smiled. I said, "My arm is hurting, can I have something for the pain?" She asked, "Would you like another shot or some pills?" Since my butt was still hurting from the last shot, I decided to take the pills. After the nurse left the room, I lay there moaning and groaning for about an hour until I fell asleep again. I awoke to the voice of a lab technician. "Good morning, Mr. Wynn. I'm here to draw some blood." I looked at the clock and said, "It's six o'clock in the morning. Besides, I gave yesterday!"

When Dr. Lewis came in to evaluate my condition, it had not improved at all. I was still running a temperature and my arm was getting bigger. This wasn't a bruise or a simple infection and I wasn't going anywhere. I was mumbling something about putting my I.V. in a back pack so that I could leave the hospital for a few hours to speak to the teachers. While I was muttering about leaving the hospital, Dr. Lewis asked if I had given a urine specimen. He had a very concerned look on his face and mentioned something about the possibility of my going into kidney failure!

Wait a minute; hold on. I bumped my arm and now you're talking about kidney failure? Did you cut class when they were studying anatomy? Before I could completely process what he had said, Dr. Lewis told the nurse that he wanted a Foley Catheter inserted. "A what?" I didn't know what it was, but it didn't sound good. The more I heard, the less I liked what I was hearing. Dr. Lewis described how they would be inserting a tube into me to allow my kidneys to drain directly. I cringed at the thought. "No, no, no. Hold on. Let me get up. I will give you a urine specimen. You are not going to..." While I protested, Dr. Lewis talked about not having any time to waste. If I was going into kidney failure, he needed to know and he wanted to know right away. "What are you talking about, kidney failure? It's my arm that's hurting." While I talked to Dr. Lewis, the nurse grabbed hold of me and inserted the catheter. "Aaaahhhhhhh. Oh God, they did it."

It all happened so quickly and unexpectedly. Now I lay there in pain from head to toe, arm swollen, unable to get up, needles in my arm and now a tube in my private parts. I had only my faith to hold on to.

*Cast thy burden upon the Lord, and He shall
sustain thee: He shall never suffer the righteous
to be moved.*
[Psalm 55:22]

Dr. Lewis told me that I would be moved to Intensive Care. My arm was in septic shock and that had pushed me to the edge of kidney failure. My blood pressure had dropped dramatically and I was still running a high temperature. My condition was to be monitored twenty-four hours a day. Needless to say, I would be missing my speaking engagement. It was finally beginning to sink in. This was serious. The Devil was busy and I needed to put on the whole armor of God to make it through.

*Put on the whole armor of God, that you may
be able to stand against the wiles of the devil.
For we wrestle not against flesh and blood, but
against principalities, against powers, against
the rulers of the darkness of this world, against
spiritual wickedness in high places.*
[Ephesians 6:11,12]

When the orderlies came to move me to Intensive Care I lay barely conscious. As they rolled me into the elevator, I looked up and saw an orderly's name tag. "Hey. How are you doing? 'Howard Benn,' you have two first names." Howard laughed and said, "You're in a good mood." I responded, "Well, I'm not going anywhere, so I may as well make the most of it. See ya later, Howard."

During the coming days I was being pushed in a wheelchair to the laboratory for one of many tests. I spoke to a young lady pushing a cart through the corridor. Although I couldn't see her badge, I later learned that her name was Michele. Michele was responsible for restocking the medicines at each of the nurses' stations. My brief encounters with Howard Benn and Michele revealed how the power of the spirit connects us one to another.

> *Comfort yourselves together, and edify*
> *one another.*
>
> [1 Thessalonians 5:11]

From that brief exchange, Howard was inspired to look in on me and keep track of my progress during my stay. Michele also kept track of my progress each day and wrote me a letter on the day of my discharge sharing how she had prayed for me since the day that I spoke to her in the corridor.

Arriving in Intensive Care, I was connected to a heart monitor. They inserted oxygen tubes into my nostrils and connected a blood pressure monitor to my right arm. I tried to raise and reposition myself in the bed with my one good arm. As I lifted myself up, I felt a sharp pain in my chest. My face went flush and I had a shortness of breath. There was a blip on the heart monitor. I was having a heart attack! As Dr. Lewis talked to me, I was responsive, but he knew that something was desperately wrong. When Dr. Lewis and the nurse left the room, I was totally exhausted and in pain. I lay there in my hospital gown just trying to process it all.

Just yesterday, I was being admitted for twenty-four hours observation. This morning, I was supposed to be speaking to teachers. Later tonight, I was suppose to get together with my sister-in-laws and their friends. What am I doing here in Intensive Care? I buzzed for the nurse. "I need something for the pain." The nurse came in and asked, "Do you want pain pills or would you rather have a shot?" I asked, "What is the difference?" She responded, "The shot is stronger and will take effect faster." Oh, this was an easy decision: "Give me a shot." Little did I know that the Demerol demons would visit me again.

When thou passest through the waters, I will be with thee; and through the rivers, they shall not overflow thee; when thou walkest through the fire, thou shalt not be burned; neither shall the flame kindle upon thee.

[Isaiah 43:2]

As I was beginning to drift off to sleep, Nina called. When I answered the telephone she asked, "How are you feeling? Why did they move you to Intensive Care?" I told her that I was all right and that I just couldn't go to the bathroom. The Demerol had me in full swing. I don't know what else Nina said. I just mumbled, "I think I had a heart attack, but that's okay because I think that I have kidney failure too. I'm hungry. Have you had dinner?" Nina was now wondering if I had lost my mind. I later learned that Nina never understood what I had said. However, feeling that something was wrong she sent everyone in her family to the hospital to see me that day.

After I hung up with Nina I lay there in bed looking up at the ceiling. The words of the song, "He's Able," by Kirk Franklin and The Family, kept running through my mind. Tears fell from my eyes; not from pain or sadness but from confidence.

*He's Able, thank you, Jesus. I know that He can
do it. He said that He'd help me through it.*

I kept repeating the words to the song over and over as I
drifted off. In my dream, I saw myself in Egypt lying on a
hillside. A young girl pointed at me and screamed in Arabic.
Everyone began pointing and hands began reaching for me. I
climbed over a wall and started running. Everyone was chasing
me and screaming. The hands were reaching for me. Finally, I
was surrounded with nowhere to go. The hands were all around
me. I was in a place of many colors and shapes. Hands reached
at me from the walls. I tried to scream, but I couldn't. I wanted
to wake up, but I couldn't. The hands just kept reaching for
me. I couldn't run. I couldn't get away. Then, finally, a hand
touched my leg.

It was the nurse waking me for medication. Praise God.
Thank you for waking me. Thank you for saving me from the
Demerol demons. She took my temperature. I lay there
sweating, my heart racing, reflecting on my nightmare. I
realized that the Demerol demons were waiting for me in my
dreams. I couldn't avoid them, so I would have to ready myself
to do battle with them the next time. They were only in my
dreams. I needed only to wake up. God would surely give me the
strength to simply wake up.

*When thou liest down, thou shalt not be afraid:
yes, thou shalt lie down, and thy sleep shall be sweet.*
[Proverbs 3:24]

The Demerol demons returned several times over the
coming days. Hands reaching for me. People chasing me,

pushing me off cliffs. Each time, I was surrounded by demonic screams. I knew that the demons couldn't hurt me, so I began to affirm each time that I felt myself falling asleep: "If God be for you, who can be against you?" [Romans 8:31].

Over the coming days I received numerous telephone calls from people who were thinking of me and praying for me. During the days that I was on Demerol, I don't remember who called, I just mumbled something each time I picked up the telephone. My mouth was dry and I couldn't seem to make any saliva. I talked as if I had cotton in my mouth. Although they don't know it, their timely telephone calls often awakened me from my dreams.

Let thy mercies come also unto me, O Lord,
even thy salvation, according to thy Word. So
shall I have wherewith to answer him that
reproacheth me: for I trust in thy Word.
[Psalm 119:41,42]

CHAPTER 6

Facing Reality

*And Solomon said, If he will show himself a
worthy man, there shall not an hair of him fall
to the earth: but if wickedness shall be found in
him, he shall die.*

[1 Kings 1:52]

The first day in the Intensive Care unit was filled with visitors. Patrice; Pam; Janice; my sisters-in-law: Brenda, Becky, and Colletha and their friends; my mother and father-in-law; and Wayne and Jacqui all came to visit. I wish that I could have taken a picture of everyone as they entered my room. Lying there with tubes running in and out of me, everyone who entered the room had an expression on their faces that screamed, "Man, you're in bad shape! We don't know if you're going to make it!" In fact, my sister-in-law, Becky, went to the pay phone when she left the room to call my wife. "Nina, you'd better get out here. Mychal is in bad shape!"

Since only two visitors were allowed at a time in Intensive Care, my visitors came in two by two. When Wayne came in, he had the same look on his face as everyone else. I guess he thought that he would cheer me up by making light of the situation. However, it was his off-centered humor that caused me unnecessary pain! Two lab technicians, Mandy and Jenny, came into the room to draw blood, but my veins kept collapsing. Each time they stuck me they were unable to hit a good vein. And, it hurt. All the while, Wayne tried to make light of it all with off the wall jokes. Although Mandy and Jenny politely laughed, they really tried to ignore Wayne while searching for a good vein. Finally, they drew blood, Wayne was quiet, and I had peace.

Over the next several days, I saw specialist after specialist. Beginning with Dr. Lewis, I was examined by Orthopedic Surgeons, Kidney Specialists, Cardiologists, and Infectious Disease Specialists. What was initially thought to be simply a bruised arm was something more. Something tragically and, possibly, terminally more.

Your faith should not stand in the wisdom of men, but in the power of God.
[1 Corinthians 2:5]

The infection in my arm led to a condition called Cellulitis. The bump with the weights was simply one in a series of unrelated events which ultimately caused the toxic infection to spread throughout my arm and threaten to destroy my entire body. Several weeks earlier, I had been bitten by a small brown spider while getting into my car. Our home is surrounded by trees and shrubbery. Insect bites and bee stings are a way of life. Just the year before, I had received over two-dozen bee stings after accidentally disturbing a bee hive while trimming my hedges. A spider bite was considered more of a nuisance than anything else. Like all of the other insect bites and bee stings in the past, I had treated the spider bite with some alcohol and gave it little attention. The bite, however, was on my elbow and never seemed to heal because I continued to bump it, one way or another.

My physical conditioning and strong immune system had fought off the potential toxic infection from the spider bite. However, bumping my arm with the weights had opened the sore yet again. The doctors *speculate* that strep bacteria entered the open sore and combined with the insect toxin. Over the next twelve hours, the combination of strep bacteria and insect toxin was rapidly spreading throughout my arm and was poisoning my entire body.

While the doctors could only *speculate* that this is how the infection began, they were sure that I had gone into septic shock. The infection in my arm had caused a high temperature and a nearly fatal collapse in blood pressure. As my body attempted to fight the poisons rapidly spreading from the infection, one by one my organs were beginning to shut down. My kidneys began to shut down and no longer accepted fluids from my body. My body attempted to reduce the spread of the infection by slowing my blood flow. The resulting low blood pressure caused a heart attack. The heart attack caused a blood clot to form on the left ventricle inside my heart. I was then in danger of the blood clot flowing through my bloodstream into my brain causing paralysis or death.

> *Turn thee unto me, and have mercy upon me;*
> *for I am desolate and afflicted.*
> [Psalm 25:16]

I had been victorious in all other areas of my life: unwavering in my faith, a good husband to my wife, good father to my children, diligent in my business allowing the anointing of the Lord to manifest itself in my writing and speaking. His power had worked through me to free parents, teachers, and their children. I was diligent in my finances and the blessings of the Lord were manifested throughout our family. I was strong. I had never been in the hospital. I was eating healthy and exercising, consistently glorifying the temple of the living God.

> *Make you perfect in every good work to do His*
> *will, working in you that which is wellpleasing*
> *in His sight, through Jesus Christ.*
> [Hebrews 13:21]

Was this an attack of the Devil or just one of those unexplainable infirmities that our frail human bodies are always susceptible to? For me, this represented the line between man's science and God's Spirit, between what we know and what we believe, and ultimately what we believe and what God says! While the doctors could *speculate* what had caused these various infirmities to come upon me, God's Word is clear. Sickness is not of God. God is light, perfection, power, and authority. To walk in God's light, according to God's plan, and obedient to God's Word, allows the Holy Spirit to dwell within us bringing to us His perfection, power, and authority. Sickness and disease are the works of the Devil. Either the Devil initiates an attack upon us, or, through our own actions or inactions we "invite" him to attack us.

*Let no man say when he is tempted, I am
tempted of God: for God cannot be tempted
with evil, neither tempteth He any man.*
[James 1:13]

I accept responsibility for having invited the Devil to attack me. Remember, for several weeks I had the spider bite that eventually provided fertile ground for the strep bacteria to enter my body. Over that period of time, I could have gone to the doctor and received treatment. Like so many others who are in good physical condition and who rarely experience sickness or ill health, we are blind to the little openings that we give the Devil. I learned through this experience that I am not indestructible, that God expects me to be responsible to His temple, and that full protection comes through obedience to His Word. That responsibility extends beyond diet and exercise to being responsible for regular physical examinations and an ongoing relationship with my doctor through his advice and counsel likened to the ongoing relationship that I have with God through prayer and meditation on His Word.

Now that I had given the Devil an opportunity to attack me, over the coming weeks, my physical condition, my positive attitude, and my faith would all be called to the test. I could have been permanently paralyzed. I could have lost my arm. I could have lost my life.

*Yea, though I walk through the valley of the
shadow of death, I will fear no evil: for thou art
with me; thy rod and thy staff they comfort me.*
[Psalm 23:4]

Over the next several days, the intravenous antibiotics had little affect on changing my condition. The blood tests weren't conclusive and Dr. Shriner, the infectious disease specialist, couldn't identify the exact cause of the infection. Was it strep or staff bacteria? Was it insect toxin? Was it a combination of bacteria and insect toxin? Whatever it was, it was stubborn. Could it be a flesh-eating bacteria eating away at my flesh from the inside?

My flesh is clothed with worms and clods of
dust; my skin is broken, and become loathsome.
[Job 7:5]

Despite the intravenous antibiotics, my arm was continuing to swell. My temperature continued to stay high and my blood pressure continued to remain low. Over the next several days, Dr. Shriner changed the mixture of antibiotics several times. Dr. Edminston, the cardiologist, put me on Heparin, a blood thinner to keep the blood clot in my heart from growing. Dr. Raj and Dr. Kumar, the kidney specialists, kept watch over me and reviewed my blood tests to ensure that I would not go into kidney failure and would not have permanent kidney damage. Over the coming weeks, there was little the team of doctors could do but wait and witness.

Wait on the Lord: be of good courage, and He shall
strengthen thine heart: wait, I say, on the Lord.
[Psalm 27:14]

Despite all of their medical expertise and knowledge, the doctors were in agreement on only one thing: they had never seen a case like this and no one could explain what, how, and why all of this was happening. However, I didn't need a medical degree to know that the Devil had invaded my body and that only the Anointed One [Christ] and his anointing could pull me through it. During the first days I would awaken throughout the night. There was plenty of time for prayer, meditation, and fellowship with God. With my swollen arm elevated on pillows, I lay on my back staring up at the ceiling or looking out of the window at the Pasadena Foothills. It was probably the third day in Intensive Care that I reconciled during my fellowship with God about 3:30 in the morning that while I trusted Him for a full recovery, I was prepared to die. I trusted God not only for a full and prosperous life here on earth, but for a joyous life everlasting.

> *For I reckon that the sufferings of this present*
> *time are not worthy to be compared with the*
> *glory which shall be revealed in us.*
> [Romans 8:18]

I reflected on the things that I had accomplished and the dreams that remained unfulfilled. While I wanted to see my sons grow up and to be a loving father, trusted friend, and wise counselor to them, I fully trusted God to provide for them in the event that I never saw them again. In fact, I laughed as I thought of how my books would skyrocket in value upon my death allowing my wife and children to become millionaires.

> *Blessed is the man that feareth the Lord, that*
> *delighteth greatly in His commandments. His*
> *seed shall be mighty upon earth: the generation*
> *of the upright shall be blessed. Wealth and riches*
> *shall be in his house: and his righteousness*
> *endureth for ever.*
> [Psalm 112:1-3]

As I reflected on the prospect of my wife and children living in prosperity and abundance from my royalties, I pleaded with God, "Please God, if my wife remarries please don't let her marry a crook!" While I knew that my wife would never allow anyone to abuse or otherwise misuse my children, I asked the Lord to send a Guardian Angel to protect them. As these thoughts went through my mind, I realized that I was at peace with my situation. When I spoke to Nina later that day, I asked her to contact our attorney to ensure that my will and other related paperwork was in order.

> *But none of these things move me, neither count*
> *I my life dear unto myself, so that I might finish*
> *my course with joy.*
>
> [Acts 20:24]

I wasn't afraid to die. I fully trusted God to protect and provide for my family should I die. However, I wasn't ready to go! I didn't want to die. I wanted to enjoy many more years of my marriage. I had spent the first nine years working everything out. I was just beginning to understand my wife. I wanted to watch my sons grow up, get married and have children. I wanted to have heart to heart talks, be part of the joy of their successes in life, go fishing, skiing, roller blading, and whatever else we could experience together. After all, Jalani was only three-years-old. He was only beginning to hang out with Mychal-David and me! The full anointing of God hadn't yet fallen upon me. There were many more books to be written, many more people to be spoken to. No, God, I am prepared, but I am not ready. There are still too many places to go, things to experience, and people to share my testimony with.

I will sing unto the Lord as long as I live: I will
sing praise to my God while I have my being.
My dedication of Him shall be sweet: I will be
glad in the Lord.
[Psalm 104:33,34]

God, indeed, showed mercy and compassion, having guided me
into the anointed hands of Dr. Lewis. Dr. Lewis was a Christian
who had planned to attend the seminary before deciding to go to
medical school. He understood that his medical knowledge could
only take him so far. He could treat each patient according to
man's limited knowledge, but that the ultimate and final healing
was always within the hands of God. Dr. Lewis told me that
when I entered Intensive Care, it was already in God's hands.

Then saith Jesus unto him, Get thee hence,
Satan: for it is written, Thou shalt worship the
Lord thy God, and Him only shalt thou serve.
Then the Devil leaveth Him, and, behold,
angels came and ministered unto Him.
[Matthew 4:10,11]

There was no clear clinical reason of how a person in my
physical condition could, in twenty-four hours, be just this
side of death. It's still difficult for me to process, "This side of
death?" I was free of the fear of death through the promise of
everlasting life. While I was in a great deal of pain, I had the
will to live. I never thought that I would die and apparently I
never felt that I was on the verge of dying.

For God so loved the world, that He gave His
only begotten Son, that whosoever believeth in
Him should not perish, but have everlasting life.
[John 3:16]

Over the next four weeks, Dr. Lewis prescribed Demerol and Vicodin to relieve the pain. The infectious disease doctors prescribed intravenous antibiotics to combat the infection. The cardiologist prescribed Heparin, a blood-thinning medication given intravenously to prevent blood clots. While on Heparin blood tests would be taken daily to regulate the dosage. Nearing my release I was moved from Heparin to Coumadin. Coumadin was also a blood-thinning medication taken orally. I learned that nearly every medication came with side effects. The Demerol brought on the demons. The antibiotics caused constipation, and with the Heparin and Coumadin I had to be careful of any cuts or bruises since the bleeding would continue much longer than normal. In fact, I got a nose bleed the second day that I was on Heparin. It seemed that my nose was going to bleed forever.

In addition to the medications, there were daily scans and examinations of my head, heart, arm, and lungs. Yet, despite the team of doctors, tests, scans, and examinations it was only God's grace and mercy that took me through it.

> *Who hath saved us, and called us with an holy calling, not according to our works, but according to His own purpose and grace, which was given us in Christ Jesus before the world began.*
> [2 Timothy 1:9]

CHAPTER 7

Humble Me before The Lord

*My son, attend to my words; incline thine ear
unto my sayings. Let them not depart from
thine eyes; keep them in the midst of thine
heart. For they are life unto those that find
them, and health to all their flesh.*
[Proverbs 4:20-22]

After days of intensive care, my condition finally stabilized. I no longer needed oxygen. I began my journey through several hospital rooms. In each room, I got to know a new group of nurses. Now that I wasn't constantly on pain medication, I spent more time talking to nurses, orderlies, doctors, and custodians. Anyone who came into my room I talked to. Anyone whom I passed in the corridor as I lay in my bed being pushed to the lab for testing I talked to. I was so happy to be among the living that I wanted to talk to everyone.

For there is no respect of persons with God.
[Romans 2:11]

Since I obviously was going to be here longer than the twenty-four hours as initially thought by Dr. Lewis, I was intent on finding joy in my situation. While my hospital care was in the hands of the doctors and nurses, my healing was in the hands of the Lord. With the pain, the catheter, my hospital gown, and lying helplessly in bed, it was clear that I wasn't in control, but more helpless than I had been since I was that undernourished, unattractive little baby given up for adoption.

While I had little control over my physical condition I had complete control over my attitude. I asked the nurse for a Bible. I talked to God and searched the scriptures daily for healing prayers. Between Demerol shots, while I was coherent, I prayed in the Spirit and had conversations with God. "Father, what would you have me learn from this situation?" The first answer that I received from God was, "Be still." That didn't tell me much, so I continued to pray hoping that God would elaborate a little more on what He wanted me to learn and perhaps, more importantly, what He wanted me to do with what I had learned.

> *Call upon me, and I will answer thee, and*
> *show thee great and mighty things, which thou*
> *knowest not.*
> [Jeremiah 33:3]

I called my wife after one of my conversations with God and told her that God had told me to be still. She asked, "Well what does that mean?" to which I responded, "I don't know, but I will get back to you after God gets back to me."

> *Our conversation is in heaven; from whence also*
> *we look for the Savior, the Lord Jesus Christ.*
> [Philippians 3:20]

The next day God spoke to me again: "Be Happy." I repeated to myself, "Be Happy." I smiled as I understood that God was telling me to be diligent and consistent. To take the same measure of faith that I had before being hospitalized and to continue in it now. There is no testimony in being happy during the good times, but there is powerful testimony in being happy during the midst of the storm! I understood what God wanted me to do, to be still and allow Him to heal my body; be happy and provide a testimony of His omnipotence power, mercy, grace, and compassion; to be consistent, to be diligent, to be still, and to be happy.

As I continued to pray and to meditate, I began to write about my experiences in the hospital. Through this challenge God was preparing me for greater things.

> *It is good for me that I have been afflicted; that*
> *I might learn thy statutes*
>
> [Psalm 119:71]

Over the coming days He not only spoke to me but sent the Holy Spirit through the gift of prophesy to my wife's aunt. My wife's aunt and I hadn't said more than two words to each other during the nine years that my wife and I had been married. It wasn't that we didn't like each other, but when I was dating my wife, her aunt felt that I had a bad spirit and I felt that she was crazy! Well, to my surprise my wife's mother called the second day that I was in Intensive Care and made a conference call. Guess who was on the other line? Everyone calls my wife's aunt, "Sister." Sister began by saying, "Hello Mychal, I heard that you were in the hospital and I just wanted to know if you would mind if I prayed for you?" I immediately said, "No Sister, I don't mind at all. Feel free to pray for me as much as you like." Sister prayed for me and with me, after which we talked for a while. I shared with her how I was not afraid or in despair. I trusted God to heal me. I also shared with her my conversations with the Lord and the things that He had instructed me to do.

Let the words of my mouth, and the meditation
of my heart, be acceptable in thy sight, Oh
Lord, my strength, and my redeemer.
[Psalm 19:14]

Sister called me nearly everyday that I was in the hospital to pray for me and with me. During that time the Lord revealed several prophesies to her. The first was that He was preparing me, through this experience, to provide testimony for His Church. In all of the speaking that I had done over the past fifteen years, I had seldom been called to speak at churches. The second prophesy was that my primary doctor, Dr. Lewis, was anointed as a minister in God's Word and that he would become a blessing to Nina and me beyond his medical expertise. In a subsequent conversation with Dr. Lewis he shared with me that he had planned to go into the ministry prior to going to medical school and that he was an ordained minister in his church. The final prophesy that Sister had was that God would be calling me into the ministry. He was preparing me with a special anointing to use for the benefit of His Church.

Having then gifts differing according to the
grace that is given to us, whether prophecy, let
us prophesy according to the proportion of faith.
[Romans 12:6]

I spent each day reading my Bible, praying, meditating, and writing. I focused my energy on what God wanted me to learn from my situation. I didn't allow time for falling into self-pity and depression. I never wondered, "why me?" I never complained about the pain or about my condition. In fact, I grew mentally, physically, and spiritually stronger each day.

A hospital can easily become a depressing place to be. After a few days, a person can lose touch with the outside world as the days and nights begin to blend together. For many, their only comfort is the television. Nothing provides relief from the crying, moaning, and screaming heard throughout the corridors. At least two people near my room passed away. I heard the crying and anguish of their families. I heard the constant screams of those who could find no relief from their pain. In the Bible, we are told that the infirmities that befell Job allowed Satan to challenge Job's faith. As Job lost his possessions and as his body was filled with suffering and disease, he was challenged to maintain his trust in God. Despite the many tragedies and the long suffering, Job stood steadfast and did not turn away from God. I was determined that not only would I maintain my faith, but that I would share my testimony over the coming days with whomever I came into contact. Anyone whom I met heard me laugh and provide testimony to God's grace and mercy.

> *We desire that every one of you do show the same*
> *diligence to the full assurance of hope unto the end.*
> *That ye be not slothful, but followers of them who*
> *through faith and patience inherit the promises.*
> [Hebrews 6:11,12]

I accepted that my body was in the hospital, but I kept my mind and my spirit in heavenly places. I filled my days with prayer, laughter, rest, meditation on God's Word, and I came to appreciate my infirmities and the experiences of each moment as important steps in my journey. People began to know me by the sounds of gospel music bellowing from my room together with the laughter that echoed throughout the corridor. I laughed and joked with my doctors as I teased them about how their enormous medical knowledge (over three hundred and fifty years of education between them) couldn't provide the answers related to my case. I told them that the blood clot in my heart would totally dissolve, and it did. I told them that I wouldn't have any permanent damage from the heart attack, and I didn't. I told the infectious disease doctors, who feared that I might have permanent loss of mobility to my left arm, that I wouldn't, and I haven't. In fact, three weeks after my release from the hospital, I was lifting weights again.

(As it is written, I have made thee a father of
many nations,) before him whom he believed,
even God, who quickeneth the dead, and calleth
those things which be not as though they were.
[Romans 4:17]

My days of stillness allowed me to pray and meditate unhindered and uninterrupted as never before. I began to understand how I had hindered God's full anointing from coming upon me as I allowed myself to be constantly distracted by the demands of family and business. I realized that in my zeal to be the best husband to my wife, best father to my children, and best businessman in my business, I was putting more focus on my efforts and less on God's guidance. I was spending so much time planning and scheduling, directing and coordinating, that I was not operating within God's plan.

Show me thy ways, Oh Lord; teach me thy paths. Lead me in thy truth, and teach me: for thou art the God of my salvation; on thee do I wait all the day.

[Psalm 25:4,5]

Our actions in the midst of the storm reveal our faith and define our character. How we handle burdens and confront obstacles provides the truest measure of who we are and what we believe. Perhaps it is these moments that provide the truest testimony of our faith and of our resolve to trust God. It's easy to trust God when the tragedies are happening to the other guy. It's easy to tell someone else to pray their way through a situation. It's easy to tell someone else to "Trust God. He will help you through it." But this wasn't happening to someone else, this was happening to me. Despite all that was happening, I still had choices. I could have chosen to feel sorry for myself. I could have chosen to be mean-spirited and upset. I could have chosen to be worried and depressed. Yes, there was plenty that I could have chosen to complain about. But I took charge of my attitude. This was the one thing that I had complete control over. I am the Captain of the ship of my attitude. I am in complete control of the direction in which my attitude sails. The wind that fills my sails are the words of my mouth. The sustenance of my spirit is within the power of my tongue. What I speak and what I affirm during the midst of the storm defines who I am.

Let no corrupt communication proceed out
of your mouth, but that which is good to the
use of edifying, that it may minister grace
unto the hearers.

[Ephesians 4:29]

My situation wasn't just a test of faith, it was a test of character, a test of focus. Would I focus on what was wrong or on what was right? Would I focus on what the doctors didn't know or on their sincerity in trying to heal me? Would I focus on the interruptions by the nurses or on the fact that when I needed them they were there? Would I focus on all of the sticking and poking by the lab technicians or on the fact that they were compassionate and knowledgeable in doing their jobs? Would I focus on the moaning, groaning, crying, and screaming of other patients or on the fact that my pain could have been much worse? Would I focus on the catheter or on the fact that I wasn't in kidney failure? Would I focus on the pain in my arm or on the joy of still having an arm? Would I focus on the disappointment of being forced to stay in the hospital or on the joy of still being alive? Would I focus on the fact that my wife wasn't here with me or on the fact that she was home with our children? Would I focus on the fact that I was hospitalized from home or on the fact that I was surrounded by the love and encouragement of dedicated doctors, nurses, orderlies, friends, and family? I learned that when you focus on God, His Word, and His promises, in the midst of darkness you can still see the light.

For I am persuaded, that neither death, nor life,
nor angels, nor principalities, nor powers, nor
things present, nor things to come, Nor height,
nor depth, nor any other creature, shall be able
to separate us from the love of God, which is in
Christ Jesus our Lord.

[Romans 8:38,39]

By keeping my focus on God and not on my situation, He gave me personal testimony to replace bitter memories. He gave me hope to replace despair. He gave me strength to replace weakness. He gave me new friends to replace disassociated doctors and nurses. Thank you Father.

Finally, my brethren, be strong in the Lord, and
in the power of his might. Put on the whole
armor of God, that ye may be able to stand
against the wiles of the devil.

[Ephesians 6:10,11]

CHAPTER 8

A Room with a View

Have faith in God. For verily I say unto you,
that whosoever shall say unto this mountain, Be
thou removed, and be thou cast into the sea;
and shall not doubt in his heart, but shall
believe that those things which he saith shall
come to pass; he shall have whatsoever he saith.
Therefore I say unto you, what things soever ye
desire, when ye pray, believe that ye receive
them, and ye shall have them.

[Mark 11:22-24]

There is no resting in Intensive Care. It is impossible to find a comfortable position with all of the wires connected to you and tubes stuck in you. There is no privacy because there is no door. There is only a curtain used to block out the light. Nothing can block out the sounds of nurses talking, patients moaning, and machines pumping and beeping. There are no flowers, no amenities. I came to view Intensive Care as the holding ground between life and death. The place where you can slip away to death or be pulled back to life. As I lay there singing to myself, the nurse pulled back my curtain. I was going to be moved out of Intensive Care. Praise God. It was time to be disconnected from the oxygen tubes, heart monitor, and the blood pressure monitor. It was time to go forth into the land of the living.

The orderlies rolled my bed into a monitored room where I made a friend in my newest nurse, Becky. Still bedridden Becky washed me with warm towels each morning as if I was a baby. Believe me, by this time I had been totally humbled. Without shame, I was simply praising God for having taken me through it all and for having blessed me with someone like Becky. I discovered that Becky was an aspiring romance novelist. I shared ideas with her about publishing her own book as a step toward fulfilling her dreams. I also introduced her to Wayne, who shared with her the ups and downs he had encountered in publishing his first book. Becky was shy about her writing, but Wayne and I both encouraged her to affirm her dreams. It is such a wonderful thing to have a dream. As Reverend Kenneth Copeland would say, "Name it and claim it, blab it and grab it." Make your requests known unto the Lord.

> *Ask, and it shall be given you; seek, and you shall find; knock, and it shall be opened unto you: For every one that asketh receiveth; and he that seeketh findeth; and to him that knocketh it shall be opened.*
>
> [Matthew 7:7,8]

After a few days in the monitored room, Becky came in one morning and told me that my condition had markedly improved. I was going to be moved from monitored care to a beautiful fourth floor room with a view of the mountains. When the orderlies moved me to the fourth-floor, it was like being moved into a hotel. The room was large with windows on one wall, running the entire length of the room. There was a VCR, refrigerator, a sofa and several chairs. And praise God, there was a bath tub. I couldn't wait to soak in a nice hot bath. I hadn't taken a bath or shower in nearly two weeks.

As I settled into my new room I learned that Dr. Lewis had ordered the nurse to take the catheter out. I cringed at the thought. I took a deep breath and before I knew it, it was over. Praise God. I was free again. I could get up without the fear of hanging the tube up on anything. I didn't have to carry my bag of urine around anymore. I was free from the catheter and about to soak in a hot bath tub. Praise God. Things were looking up.

My arm was healing and Dr. Lewis felt that it was okay to put it in a sling and to walk around the room. The nurse disconnected the I.V.s, wrapped my arm with plastic, so that I wouldn't get water into the I.V. lines, and I took a nice long hot bath. I soaked for nearly two hours.

How great are His signs! And how mighty are His wonders! His kingdom is an everlasting kingdom, and His dominion is from generation to generation.

[Daniel 4:3]

After my bath, I settled into my bed, relaxed and smelling good. There was joy in my heart as I felt God healing and strengthening me. I called Nina and we began making plans for her to come to get me. Dr. Shriner, the infectious disease specialist, advised me not to fly back to Atlanta. She was concerned that the pressurized air cabin could provide a catalyst for any lingering infection and cause my arm to become inflamed again. She felt that the two weeks that it had taken to reduce the infection and swelling in my arm could all be reversed. Nina and I decided to have her father fly from Los Angeles to Atlanta to help her make the drive across country. He, Nina, and our two sons would make the twenty-two hundred mile trip from Atlanta to Los Angeles to take me home.

We were back on schedule. Nina and I were already looking beyond my release from the hospital and resuming our business. Nina had rescheduled the speaking engagement that I had missed in Austin, Texas, so that I could speak in Austin on the way back to Atlanta. We would continue from Austin to Columbia, South Carolina, where I would speak at a church-sponsored conference. We had everything planned. Even if I had to speak from a wheel chair, I wasn't going to miss any more speaking engagements. Satan was not going to hinder me from sharing God's anointed message.

I was anxious to see my family and my wife and children were anxious to see me. I felt strong in my Spirit and confident that my body was being made perfect in its healing. It wouldn't be long now. I was intent on being awake in the morning to watch the breaking of the new day over the mountains. The words of the song, "No Weapon Formed Against Me Shall Prosper" rang in my ears as I fell asleep. From the brink of death, God was healing me, revealing His purpose to me, preparing me. No weapon formed against me shall prosper.

Well, my room with a view lasted for only a day. The next morning, before I could take my bath, the nurse told me that they were going to move me again. After only one joy-filled day in my fourth floor suite, I discovered that they would be moving me to the second floor. They gathered up all of my things and loaded them onto the bed with me. Like a homeless person pushing all of his earthy belongings in a cart, all of my possessions rode with me on my bed. This was a busy day at the hospital and I was being moved to the busiest floor. The orderlies pushed me into a tiny second floor room. They set all of my belongings, including my bags of chips, flowers, books, and cards on the floor. My wall of windows overlooking the mountains was replaced with a single window that overlooked the back alley of the hospital. I just closed my eyes, lay back, and went to sleep.

And it shall come to pass, if ye shall hearken diligently unto my commandments which I command you this day, to love the Lord your God, and to serve Him with all your heart and with all your soul, That I will give you the rain of your land in His due season, the first rain and the latter rain, that thou mayest gather in thy corn, and thy wine, and thine oil. And I will send grass in thy fields for thy cattle, that thou mayest eat and be full.
[Deuteronomy 11:13-15]

CHAPTER 9

Yet Another Test

*Out of the depths have I cried unto thee, O
Lord. Lord, hear my voice: let thine ears be
attentive to the voice of my supplications...
I wait for the Lord, my soul doth wait,
and in His Word do I hope.*

[Psalm 130:1,5]

The nurse woke me for dinner. She hardly had any room to put down my dinner tray. After she left, I got out of bed determined to make the best of a bad situation. I hadn't complained, been depressed, been discouraged, or felt sorry for myself through this entire ordeal. I wasn't going to allow this room to depress me. I pushed my dinner tray aside. Dragging my I.V. machine, I began to rearrange my room. Weakly, I struggled to pick my things up off of the floor with my one good arm. Just as I was stumbling along, Patrice came in. She laughed at me as she ushered me back into bed. With me directing, she rearranged everything. She set up my music, arranged my flowers in front of my bed, pushed the other bed over to allow more room for my trays. With my direction and Patrice's effort, we made my room much more functional and comfortable. Oh, what a blessing. Patrice, God's ministering angel, was here again, right on time.

After Patrice left, I drifted off to sleep. I was awakened by the screams of a lady in the room across from me. She cried over and over, "Help me, help me, help me." The nurses were doing all that they could, but nothing seemed to ease her pain. I prayed for her before I asked the nurse to close my door so that I could get some sleep.

I spent the next few days on the second floor. The infection in my arm was still causing me to run an occasional fever. Each night I awakened between two and four o'clock in the morning soaking wet with my arm in pain. I would lay awake thinking about getting back to the business of being a husband to my wife and a father to my sons. God hadn't brought me this far to fail me now.

I am weary with my groaning; all the night
make I my bed to swim; I water my couch with
my tears.

[Psalm 6:6]

Today was two weeks from the day that I had come to Los Angeles for a three-day stay. Nina was going to be leaving Atlanta today. They would drive up through Memphis to have dinner with my mother and allow her some time to visit with her grandchildren. There was more good news today as they were reopening the fourth floor and I was going to be moved back to my fourth floor suite.

Perfect! When Nina and the boys get here I will have plenty of room. The boys can watch their videos, I'll have a refrigerator, and we will have a good time. I could hardly wait. I hadn't held my wife in over two weeks. I was definitely in the mood for romance even though in my condition there was little that I could do! And my boys, they needed to see me and I needed to see them. They had handled this so well, but they needed to see their daddy.

Dr. Lewis expected to release me within the next three days. That would give us ample time to get to Austin, Texas, and then on to Columbia, South Carolina for my presentations. Yes, we were back on schedule, ready to rock and roll. Thank you, Father. I'm ready to get back to business.

I felt so good that I thought I would get out of bed and sit in a chair. I had a gospel tape playing as I settled back into a big comfortable chair. It was a beautiful Southern California day. There was a beautiful blue sky cleansed by the winds. I walked around singing and praising God. He'd taken me through the storm. My family was on their way and in a few days I would be released from the hospital. Thank you, Father. I couldn't wait to provide testimony of His grace and mercy. I had a powerful testimony to share. I planned to tell people about the power of God and the blessings that accompany one's faithfulness to His Word.

After lunch, the nurse disconnected my I.V.s. They had discontinued the Heparin and I wouldn't need any further antibiotics until later that night. I was free! No catheter. No I.V. I couldn't wait to slip into another hot bath. I filled the bath tub with baby shampoo to create a lot of bubbles. I must have soaked for nearly an hour. Just as I was finishing, Dr. Lewis came in to discuss my forthcoming release. I wrapped a bath towel around me, walked out into the room and stood next to Dr. Lewis. He and I talked, and I was feeling pretty good about myself when I let out a screech. In that moment, my right leg wobbled and then the entire right side of my body collapsed. If not for Dr. Lewis grabbing my right arm I would have fallen with my full weight onto the floor. I sat on the floor expressionless. Dr. Lewis was asking me, "Mychal, are you okay? What happened? Can you talk?"

While I heard Dr. Lewis, I couldn't find the words to respond. Dr. Lewis asked me again, "Mychal, is everything okay?" Finally, I looked at Dr. Lewis and said, "If everything was okay I wouldn't be sitting on the floor. I can't move my leg." Dr. Lewis called a nurse and they helped me into the bed. They connected me to oxygen and a heart monitor. Although every one was busily working around me, things appeared to be moving in slow motion. I could feel Dr. Lewis touch my right leg. "Mychal, can you feel that?" I just nodded my head. "Wiggle your toes." Dr. Lewis, repeated himself. "Mychal, can you wiggle your toes?" I lay there looking at my toes. I was telling my toes to move but nothing happened. "Mychal, can you move your leg?" I just sat there and shook my head. My toes wouldn't wiggle. My leg wouldn't move. Oh, God.

Trust in the Lord with all thine heart; and lean
not unto thine own understanding. In all thy ways
acknowledge Him, and He shall direct thy paths.
[Proverbs 3:5,6]

They rushed me into Intensive Care. People were all around me, making a fuss. With oxygen tubes in my nose, a blood pressure monitor on my right arm, a heart monitor connected to my chest, they worked on me. Nina called to tell me that her and the boys were outside of Memphis. Dr. Lewis took the call and told her that I'd had a stroke. With Nina holding on one telephone Dr. Lewis was speaking with the head of Neurology at the USC Medical Center in Los Angeles. They were discussing moving me by helicopter to the USC Neurology Unit for immediate surgery. Dr. Lewis feared that the blood clot had gone into my brain and that a surgical procedure would be needed within the hour to save my life.

Oh God, why now? I had done all that I could to assure Nina that everything was alright and that she didn't need to worry; that everything was in God's hands and that I was being healed in accordance with His Word. Tears streamed down my face as I worried about what Nina must be thinking. She had over a two-day drive ahead of her and now she was being told that her husband had had a stroke, was back in Intensive Care, and may require brain surgery.

> *The Lord is my rock, and my fortress, and my*
> *deliverer; my God, my strength, in whom I will*
> *trust; my buckler, and the horn of my salvation,*
> *and my high tower. I will call upon the Lord,*
> *who is worthy to be praised: so shall I be saved.*
> [Psalm 18:2,3]

Twenty minutes later, I regained some muscular control in my leg. While it was still very weak, I could wiggle my toes and raise my leg a little. Dr. Lewis let out a sigh of relief. They wouldn't need to do surgery. Later that day my wife's family came to visit. Her parents, sisters, nieces and nephews all came. My wife had called everyone following her conversation with Dr. Lewis. "Go out to the hospital and see what's wrong with my husband!"

Notwithstanding the Lord stood with me, and strengthened me.

[2 Timothy 4:17]

The clinical diagnosis was that a portion of the blood clot in my heart had broken away and had gone into my brain causing a stroke. The blood clot didn't show up on a brain scan the next day, so the neurologist felt that the clot had dissolved. An echocardiogram was run that revealed both good and bad news. The good news was that the blood clot remaining in my heart was significantly smaller (as a result of a large piece having broken away causing the stroke)! The bad news was that if any more of the clot broke away it could cause permanent paralysis or death.

After each of the respective specialists had come in to give me their assessment; I closed my eyes and asked, "Father what are you trying to tell me?" I lay there in my bed with my eyes closed waiting and believing for an answer. My mind was off the stroke, off the blood clot, off the tubes in my nose and off of the pain in my arm. I was just waiting for an answer. I suddenly heard the words, "Be still, My Son. Be Still?" I immediately understood that up until the stroke I was still on my time. I had defeated the works of the Devil and I was already concerned with not missing my next speaking engagements. I was already planning and orchestrating. Nina and I were proceeding like nothing had happened. Nina was operating on what I had told her. "I'm okay, honey. My arm had a slight infection but it's okay now." God had saved my arm, pulling me back from the brink of death. He had revealed to me a prophesy that I would be called to provide testimony of His grace and mercy and I was still behaving as if everything was "okay." The doctors had told me that it wasn't okay and now God was revealing to me that it wasn't okay. I was being prepared for kingdom business. It was time for me to "Be Still."

> *Judge me, O Lord; for I have walked in mine integrity: I have trusted also in the Lord; therefore I shall not slide.*
>
> [Psalm 26:1]

I wasn't going to speak next week in Austin. I wasn't going to speak next week in Columbia. However, according to God's time, when I speak next I will be speaking with greater power and authority, providing testimony to His grace and mercy. Maybe I was in Intensive Care today, but at some point I would rise up, for He would not forsake me. I serve a magnificent, merciful, compassionate God. Through my obedience, I am blessed in everything that I do. I kept repeating the words of the song to myself, "He's able. I know that He can do it. He said He'd take me through it. He's able."

> *And they that know thy name will put their trust in thee: for thou, Lord, hast not forsaken them that seek thee.*
>
> [Psalm 9:10]

The next morning, Nina called and told me that they were going through Albuquerque, New Mexico. They had been driving straight through since receiving the news of my stroke. Her faith was strong and she wasn't worried. When she called later that day, she spoke to the nurse and told her that she was nearing the California border and that she expected to get to Los Angeles later that night.

Later that night my teenage niece and nephew were visiting when the neurologist came in. Without acknowledging that they were in the room, he simply interrupted our conversation and began talking. During his conversation and ensuing examination of my leg, my niece's pager went off. My niece and nephew are a part of the hip-hop generation. My nephew had several earrings in each ear. My niece had long braids and six inch heels. When her pager went off, I laughed and asked what she needed with a pager? However, I noticed that the neurologist had interrupted his examination and was giving her a long cold stare, the kind of stare that they give black children in stores. The kind of stare that people give black children, not because they're children, but because they're black children.

> *Whosoever shall offend one of these little ones*
> *[children] that believe in me, it is better for*
> *him that a millstone were hanged about his*
> *neck, and he were cast into the sea.*
> [Mark 9:42]

My conversation with the neurologist went downhill from there. When he finally stopped staring at my niece, he casually mentioned that "they," meaning the cardiologist, would probably want to put a tube down my throat [Transesophageal Echocardiogram] to look at my heart. When I asked him why, he told me in a condescending tone of voice that, "Well in medicine, we want to gather as much information as we possibly can..." I waited until he was done with his lecture and asked, "Well, what type of information could you obtain from the tube in my throat that you don't already know? And, what changes in my treatment could result from any additional information that you might gain?" He looked at me for a moment like something was wrong with me for asking for a further explanation, and without answering my question he appealed to my ego. "Well, you're a business man. I'm sure that you try to gain as much information as you can before making major decisions regarding your business. If it was me, I would have the procedure done." After he was finished, I thanked him and resumed my conversation with my niece and nephew. I'm sure that they hadn't noticed the look that he had given them, but it was something that I couldn't forget.

> *Get behind me, Satan: thou art an offence unto me: for thou savourest not the things that be of God, but those that be of men.*
> [Matthew 16:23]

After everyone had left, I went over in my mind the entire situation with the neurologist, putting together little bits and pieces of his conversation, how he had looked at my niece and nephew, and how he hadn't acknowledged them when he entered the room. I reflected on his conversation with me and the comments that he had made about my primary physician, Dr. Lewis. The more I thought about it, the angrier I got. Finally, I lay back and prayed that God would reveal to me how He wanted me to handle this situation. In even the most insignificant dealings with others, when God is invited to work with the problem, revelation knowledge will come.

One of the nurses came in and we talked for a while. I shared with her the situation that had occurred with the neurologist. As I talked about what had happened, the answer was revealed to me, "Take him off your case. Don't be angry. Just remove him from your team of physicians." I decided to share my concerns with Dr. Lewis and to have the neurologist removed from my case. However, I had something more important to deal with now. I told the nurse that I wanted her to call Dr. Lewis to let him know that I wanted to be transferred out of Intensive Care. My wife and sons would be there later today and I refused to be in a bed in Intensive Care when they got there. Besides, only two visitors at a time were allowed in Intensive Care and children under the age of twelve were not allowed at all. Well, that just wasn't going to do. I wanted to be transferred out, first thing that morning.

God told me to be still, but I could be still in another room where my children could visit me. I wanted the nurse to call Dr. Lewis right then, at 3:00 A.M.! She got me to agree to allow her to wait until 5:30 A.M. Dr. Lewis later shared with me how he had been "On Call" and awake much of the previous night and that when he received a telephone call at 5:30 A.M. from a nurse asking for orders to move a patient to another room, he almost exploded. But God calmed his spirit and he simply told the nurse that it was okay to move me out of Intensive Care.

> *He that is slow to anger is better than the mighty; and he that ruleth his spirit than he that taketh a city.*
> [Proverbs 16:32]

CHAPTER 10

Time to Wait and be Healed

*I wait for the Lord, my soul doth wait, and in
His Word do I hope.*

[Psalm 130:5]

R ight after lunch, they moved me from Intensive Care to a nice
little room, and I do mean "little." Here I was again, stuck
in a little room, yet it didn't matter as long as I was able to see
my wife and children. The nurses, however, were looking out for
me "Mychal, don't worry. There will be a larger room available
later today. It's really nice, and your children will have room to play."
Remember, with my positive attitude and compassionate spirit,
I had sown good seeds with all of the doctors, nurses, and hospital
staff since being admitted. People caring about, praying for, and
looking out for me was a part of the harvest that God had promised.

*Be not deceived; God is not mocked: for whatsoever
a man soweth, that shall he also reap.*

[Galatians 6:7]

When Nina, her sister, Brenda, and my two sons arrived, I
expected my children to run over and shower me with love.
This was not quite the case. When they entered the room,
Mychal-David stopped at the doorway and just stared. He
stared first at the sight of the I.V.s in my right arm and then

ran his eyes across my body to my left arm which was hidden beneath the sheet. I said, "Hi Mychal-David. How are you?" He responded, "Fine." I said, "Come on in and give me a hug." As he slowly walked toward me, he stopped at the foot of the bed and said, "Dad, let me see your arm." Before I could pull my arm from beneath the sheet, my three-year-old son, Jalani, must have felt that Mychal-David was moving too slow. Jalani said, "Hi Daddy," pushed past Mychal-David, and jumped into the bed with me. When I pulled my left arm out, Mychal-David said, "Dad, your skin is peeling like a snake." Jalani jumped in and said, "A spider bite you?" I began laughing with my spider-bitten snake arm!

After hugging Mychal-David, I finally embraced my wife. It had only been sixteen days since I last held her. However, a lot had happened during those sixteen days. It wasn't long before Mychal-David and Jalani were ready to go. They had seen daddy, they had seen the spider-bitten snake arm. Daddy was okay. Time to go to McDonald's.

Dr. Lewis sat down with Nina and me and shared with Nina the entire chain of events from our first meeting in his office to the stroke. Following which, he told us that he wasn't going to release me until the blood clot in my heart had completely dissolved. He didn't know how long it would take. It could be anywhere from a few days to a few weeks, to a month or more. He said that he understood that it would be a financial strain on us, but that at this point it was entirely in God's hands.

God shall supply all your need according to His riches in glory by Christ Jesus.
[Philippians 4:19]

While others would have listened to Dr. Lewis with unbelieving ears, Nina and I simply laughed with him. We were all in agreement. This was in God's hands. My healing, our finances, everything was in God's hands. Dr. Lewis, Nina, and I were all in agreement that God's grace and mercy would take us through it.

> *Again I say unto you, That if two of you shall agree on earth as touching any thing that they shall ask, it shall be done for them of my Father which is in heaven. For where two or three are gathered together in my name, there am I in the midst of them.*
>
> [Matthew 18:19,20]

After meeting with Dr. Lewis, Nina and I resolved that she and Mychal-David would fly back to Atlanta the following weekend. We accepted that when Dr. Lewis was confident that God had healed me, Nina would fly back to Los Angeles and that we would drive back to Atlanta. Nina didn't want to leave without me. Her mission was to come here and take her husband back home. However, we had prayed together and we knew that we were on God's time, not our time.

As promised, the nurses moved me to a larger room and brought in a bed for Nina. Over the next several days, Nina stayed with me. I had an opportunity to see my boys. We even had a pizza party one night with friends and family. Each day I was getting stronger and God's purpose for my life was becoming clearer and clearer. Nina met nurse after nurse and doctor after doctor who told her of my attitude while I had been in the hospital. My attitude provided testimony to God's grace and mercy. My faith had never wavered. My belief in His omnipotent power and grace was never shaken, not by the infection, not by the pitiful way that I looked after days in Intensive Care, not by the heart attack, not even by the unexpected stroke. My attitude was the same throughout. God will heal me. God will reveal his purpose to me. God will use me.

> *The spirit of a man will sustain his infirmity.*
> [Proverbs 18:14]

My wife and I spent some quality time together over the next several days. She bathed me. She rubbed me down with scented lotion. She bought me pajamas. She and I stayed up each night talking.

> *Let him kiss me with the kisses of his mouth: for*
> *thy love is better than wine. Because of the*
> *savour of thy good ointments thy name is as*
> *ointment poured forth.*
> [Songs of Solomon 1:2,3]

Nina met Dr. Pamela Powell. We had a good time listening to Pamela's recant of the events the day that I spoke to the teachers. As she spoke about the concern of everyone around me, Nina and I laughed ourselves silly. Pamela shared how I went on telling my stories and talking to teachers while she, Pat, and Patrice were concerned about getting me to the doctor. It seems silly in retrospect to think that I was so wrapped up in what I was doing that I ignored all of the signs that my body was giving me that all was not well. While Pamela was talking to Nina I sat there and thought, "God does everything in an orderly manner and it was certainly not in divine order that I ignored my body's telling me that it was time to stop and be healed. As they say, "God looks out for children and fools."

Let all things be done decently and in order.
[1 Corinthians 14:40]

Over the next several days, I gave away autographed copies of my book of inspirational poetry, *"Don't Quit,"* to each of the people whom I had come to know during my time at the hospital. I signed books for doctors, nurses, orderlies, and custodians. As different people came into my room, they all seemed to have stories to share with Nina. We were one big multicultural family: black, white, Chinese, German, Philippino, West Indian, Japanese, Italian, Irish, Jewish, Armenian, and only God knows what else.

Dr. Edminston, one of the cardiologists, came in to share the results of the last echocardiogram. It was three weeks to the day that I had entered the hospital for "twenty-four hours" observation. Dr. Edminston nearly danced into the room as he announced, "I have some good news. The blood clot in your heart is almost gone. We are going to do another 'echo' next Monday by which time I expect it to be fully dissolved. You will probably be released no later than next Wednesday." I just smiled and said, "I told you so."

...O Daniel, servant of the living God, is thy
God, whom thou servest continually, able to
deliver thee from the lions? Then said Daniel
unto the king, O king, live for ever. My God
hath sent His angel, and hath shut the lions'
mouths, that they have not hurt me...
[Daniel 6:20-22]

CHAPTER II

What I Learned from Job

And Satan answered the Lord and said, "Skin for skin, yes, all that a man has will he give for his life. But put forth thine hand now and touch his bone and his flesh, and he will curse thee to thy face."

[Job 2:4,5]

D r. McIntyre, a blood specialist, joined the team. That made a total of fifteen doctors working on my case. Dr. McIntyre had reviewed my records and the notes of the other doctors. When he entered the room, he introduced himself and said, "Man, you've been through a lot." He mentioned that after reviewing my records, that the one consistent comment made by all of the doctors was, "The patient has a very positive attitude and is always in very good spirits." I laughed when Dr. McIntyre shared this with me and issued the call, "God is good," to which Dr. McIntyre responded, "All the time." Like Dr. Lewis, Dr. McIntyre knew that everything was in God's hands.

Dr. McIntyre had come to evaluate my blood tests. He was to assess whether or not my blood had a propensity to form clots or whether the clotting was just an isolated, unexplainable phenomenon. I discovered that it was Dr. McIntyre who ordered the six vials of blood drawn the night before. He was awaiting those test results but wanted to discuss with me the complete scope of what could happen upon my release. The worst case was that I might be required to have a permanent I.V. inserted into my arm to receive Heparin injections (to prevent blood clotting) for the rest of my life. In the middle of the spectrum, I might simply need to take Coumadin for a few weeks or months. At the other end of the spectrum, I might be completely healed and require nothing at all. As Dr. McIntyre shared the range of possibilities with me, I couldn't help but explode in laughter. I told him that I appreciated his sharing with me the complete range of possibilities. The information had simply given me specific requests to be made known unto God. However, prayers of complete healing had already been spoken. The healing had been received. The doctors just didn't know it!

Dr. McIntyre and I went on talking and laughing for a while. He mentioned how he had noted several interesting parallels between my situation and that of the Old Testament story of Job. I told him that while I had heard several sermons based on the book of Job, I had only read those scriptures referred to in the sermons that I had heard. Dr. McIntyre talked about how despite his long suffering, Job never turned away from God, very much like my attitude toward the various medical complications that I had experienced during my time in the hospital. If doctors had examined Job, they would have been just as baffled as the doctors on my case regarding the cause of his sickness.

After Dr. McIntyre left, I picked up my Bible, thoughtfully and diligently read through the entire forty-two chapters of the book of Job. This Old Testament account of the relationship between Job and God is forty-two chapters of difficult Old English reading. Over the next several days, I read through all forty-two chapters several times. Each reading expanded my knowledge and understanding of what was happening between Job, those around him, God, and Satan.

> *There was a man in the land of Uz, whose name was Job; and that man was perfect and upright, and one that feared God, and eschewed evil.*
>
> [Job 1:1]

I saw within the story of Job many parallels in my own life. As I had been told in the many sermons that I had heard, Job, was in fact long-suffering, yet steadfast in his faith. The account of Job revealed that he was not only perfect and upright, but through his favor with God had accumulated great wealth and was considered, "The Greatest of all the Men of the East." He was obedient to the Lord. He demonstrated wisdom and compassion to those around him. He was a good father and a good husband.

Like Job, I had found favor in the Lord as He had anointed my writing and speaking. I had been a good husband to my wife and good father to my children. Like Job, I had achieved a measure of respect in my profession. Indeed, God had blessed my faithfulness. As I stated earlier, before my infection, I was in the best health of my life and Nina and I were prospering in our business. Everything was going just fine in my life when the infection in my arm had suddenly and unexpectedly come upon me.

So went Satan forth from the presence of the
Lord, and smote Job with sore boils from the
sole of his foot unto his crown.

[Job 2:7]

As Job contemplated what had brought his illness upon him, so too did I. As Job's friends tried to reason why he was stricken, so too did my doctors attempt to reason why I had suffered so. Just as Job's friends struggled for answers, so too did my doctors.

What knowest thou, that we know not? What
understandeth thou, which is not in us?

[Job 15:9]

This, however, is where Job and I had very different perspectives regarding the cause and source of our respective afflictions. Job, believing that he was perfect and upright questioned why God had done this to him. What had he done to cause God to afflict him so? He even longed to die in order to end the affliction, even questioning the value of having ever been born.

On the other hand, while I believe that God allows us to go through certain experiences, He is not the author but the Redeemer. God did not put me through this but "allowed" me to go through it, knowing that within me was the power to get through it all. I never felt sorry for myself, pitied myself, or questioned God. Unlike Job, I knew Jesus as my Redeemer and stood steadfast on the promises.

CHAPTER 12

The Final Days

I waited patiently for the Lord; and
He inclined unto me, and heard my cry.
He brought me up also out of an horrible
pit, out of the miry clay, and set my feet
upon a rock, and established my goings.
And He hath put a new song in my mouth,
even praise unto our God: many shall see it,
and fear, and shall trust in the Lord.
                                        [Psalm 40:1-3]

Nina and Mychal-David were all set to fly back to Atlanta, even though neither of them wanted to go. Jalani was going to stay in Long Beach with Nina's relatives. Nina and I went for a walk down to the end of the floor. What a sight we made (me in my pajamas pulling the I.V. machine), Nina, as fine as she wanted to be, with her chiseled body, holding my hand, helping my pathetic looking self down the corridor. People were probably wondering, "Who is that fine looking woman with that old man?" I didn't care what they thought. While this was a far cry from the three miles that Nina and I ran each morning alongside the Chattahoochee River, Oh God, it felt so good to be up walking with my wife.

I had been in the hospital for twenty-three days. Nina and Mychal-David were leaving. She and the boys came by to say good-bye, or as my mother always taught me to say when I was growing up, "I'll see you later." Nina was really saddened that she was going to be returning to Atlanta without me. Saying good-bye again was a challenge for both of us. I tried to reassure her that these would be the final days. While the doctors still didn't know when I would be released, I was not anxious but confident that these were my last days.

Two major tests had been scheduled that would determine how much longer I would be in the hospital. Dr. Shriner, the infectious disease specialist, ordered a Gallium scan. This would show any areas of my body where infection was still concentrated. I fully expected that nothing would show up on the scan since my body was healed. Dr. Shriner laughed when I told her this, but I remained confident that God and I would have the last laugh. Dr. Edminston, the cardiologist, ordered another echocardiogram. We both agreed that we expected to see the blood clot completely gone and my heart healthy.

> *Who His own self bare our sins in His own*
> *body on the tree, that we, being dead to sins,*
> *should live unto righteousness: by whose stripes*
> *ye were healed.*
>
> [1 Peter 2:24]

Just before Nina and the boys left, a lab technician came into my room holding a large container. He told me that he had to make sure that there were no pregnant women in the area because the container contained radioactive material. He asked the nurse to disconnect my I.V. so that he could inject me with radioisotopes. What? Had he lost his mind? He said that this was part of the Gallium test. He would inject me with the radioisotopes and on each of the next three days they would perform the Gallium scans. Dr. Shriner hadn't said anything about radioactive material. I stood there looking at this lab technician holding this canister like he's carrying plutonium. I wasn't the only one noticing that there was something wrong with this picture as my eight-year-old son, Mychal-David, left the room. I told the technician that I didn't have any intention of letting him light me up with any radioactive material. The nurse, noticing my distress said that she would call Dr. Lewis. I told her that she could call whomever she wanted to. My wife's parting words as she and the boys left to go to the airport were, "You had better be careful about them injecting you with that stuff. I heard that it can make you impotent!"

A short time later, Dr. Lewis called to ask why I was refusing to take the injection. I told him that my wife told me that it could cause impotence. After a good laugh Dr. Lewis and I had a long and engaging conversation. He assured me that the test was safe and that it would be helpful in diagnosing whether there was any lingering infection in my heart or in my arm. He went on to say that this was important in determining when I could be released from the hospital. I protested by saying that we could forego the test and I was willing to stay in the hospital as long as he wanted me to. Eventually, Dr. Lewis convinced me to have the test done. After hanging up with Dr. Lewis, I took some time in prayer for further confirmation that it would be okay to agree to the test. I didn't receive a response from God one way or the other so I just prayed that the test would be done in accordance with His divine order.

*The Lord is my helper, and I will not fear what
man shall do unto me.*

[Hebrews 13:6]

Following this, I told the nurse to have the lab technician come back for the injection. It was still unsettling to watch him carry this huge, futuristic container into the room. When he opened the container, it revealed a relatively small syringe. It was like pulling a pencil out of a liter bottle of soda. After giving me the injection, he put the syringe back into its huge container and disappeared from my room. Would he be back the next day to see if I glowed?

On my twenty-fifth day in the hospital, Jacklin came in to do my echocardiogram for the fourth time. She was last here four days ago. Nina had watched the monitor during the last test as Jacklin pointed out the blood clot that was only a fraction of it's original size. The echocardiogram machine had a video monitor that allowed Jacklin to look at the function of the heart muscle, the opening and closing of the heart valves, and the overall condition of the heart. She was checking for any clotting in the left ventricle. The monitor showed that the clot was completely gone.

> *He staggered not at the promise of God through
> unbelief; but was strong in faith, giving glory to
> God; And being fully persuaded that, what He
> had promised, He was able also to perform.*
> [Romans 4:20,21]

I wasn't surprised at all because I had told Jacklin and Nina that the blood clot would be totally dissolved by today's test. I was so confident that the clot would be gone that I didn't even bother watching the monitor. I just talked to Jacklin as though we were walking in the park. She had such a beautiful heavenly smile. "Do you ever wear contact lenses? Do you cook? What's your favorite dish? Do you like riding bicycles or roller blading or skiing?" Jacklin performed her examination for about half an hour patiently answering all of my questions.

While Jacklin continued the examination, I began reminiscing on how it was this same examination that revealed a large blood clot in my heart's left ventricle nearly three weeks ago. It was a piece of that same clot that had broken away to cause the stroke twelve days ago. My reflection was interrupted when Jacklin said, "Well, Mychal, I don't see any clotting." She simply reaffirmed what God had already revealed to me. I was nearly through the valley.

For our light affliction, which is but for a moment, worketh for us a far more exceeding and eternal weight of glory; While we look not at the things which are seen, but at the things which are not seen: for the things which are seen are temporal; but the things which are not seen are eternal.
[2 Corinthians 4:17,18]

Nina called while Jacklin was doing her examination. She and Nina talked briefly. Nina had gotten to know all of my nurses, doctors, and lab technicians. In fact I had to rush one of the nurses, Maria, off of the telephone the night before because she and Nina were carrying on as if they were talking from across town rather than from across the country. I hung up the telephone with Nina before Jacklin was finished with her examination but I'm sure that Nina already knew in her spirit that God had healed me.

After Jacklin left, Richard, one of the cardiologist's Physician's Assistants, came in with the good news. The results of the echocardiogram and Gallium scans confirmed what I had already affirmed. The blood clot had completely disappeared. The infection in my body was gone. I laughed hysterically when I saw Dr. Shriner. I testified to God's omnipotent healing power. It was time for me to go home. She told the nurses to disconnect the antibiotic I.V. Richard had the nurse discontinue the Heparin. That's it. No more I.V.s. Richard and I laughed and talked a while about how little the doctors had known about my condition and why I had experienced the cellulitis in my arm, the kidney problems, the heart attack, or the resulting blood clot. Now, nearly four weeks from the day that I had been admitted, all of the cardiologists, infectious disease specialists, kidney specialists, neurologists, orthopedic specialists, and the blood specialist, were all still at a loss about exactly what had happened to me and why it had happened. They all simply shared in my joy that I was nearly through the valley, that the healing power of God was working miracles within me.

He sent His word, and healed them, and
delivered them from their destructions.
[Psalm 107:20]

I had to take one more test to confirm that there was no lingering infection in my heart. Even before the results of this final test came in, I simply affirmed, "By His Stripes I am Healed." Praise God. And of course, the test revealed no remaining infection in my heart! I put on my Chicago Bulls cap and my Calvin Klein robe and took a walk around the hospital. I took a stack of *"Don't Quit"* books with me and stopped on each floor to give away and autograph books.

> *Give, and it shall be given unto you; good*
> *measure, pressed down, and shaken together,*
> *and running over, shall men give into your*
> *bosom. For with the same measure that ye mete*
> *withal it shall be measured to you again.*
>
> [Luke 6:38]

After making my way back down to the first floor, I walked outside and sat down. It had been nearly a month since I'd had an opportunity to simply sit outside. The warm rays of the sun caressed my face. Oh God, how good it feels to sit still and appreciate the beauty of your creation.

Dr. Lewis finally came over to sign my walking papers. He is truly one of God's anointed and has been a blessing to me and to my family throughout this ordeal. He made me promise to come to his office on Friday for one final examination before I hit the road, exactly four weeks and one day since it all began. Praise God that His grace and mercy brought me through it. I wouldn't change anything that has happened. I am a better and stronger person. My wife is a better and stronger person. I have had an opportunity to touch so many lives, not from a podium, but up close and personal. Thank you, Father.

> *All things work together for good to them that*
> *love God, to them who are the called according*
> *to His purpose.*
>
> [Romans 8:28]

CHAPTER 13

Time to Renew My Strength

They that wait upon the Lord shall renew their strength; they shall mount up with wings as eagles; they shall run, and not be weary; and they shall walk, and not faint.
[Isaiah 40:31]

I spoke with my wife's sisters, Becky and Colletha, who were planning to come and drive me to Wayne's. Colletha had told me that they would be coming to the hospital between one and two o'clock in the afternoon. However, at six o'clock, they still hadn't gotten there, so I told Colletha that I didn't need them to come. I would drive myself. After my conversation with Colletha, I had one of the orderlies, John, help me put the things that I had accumulated over the course of my four weeks into my Suburban. I walked over to the pharmacy to fill my prescriptions. The pharmacy was located in a building across the street from the hospital. I had to walk down one flight of stairs and across a parking lot to get to the pharmacy. After filling my prescription, I walked back to my room and fell across the bed. I called Colletha, "I think you and Becky need to come and get me. I just walked to the pharmacy and I don't think I can drive anywhere. I don't care what time you get here, just come!"

The steps of a good man are ordered by the
Lord: and He delighteth in his way. Though he
fall, he shall not be utterly cast down: for the
Lord upholdeth him with His hand.
[Psalm 37:23,24]

After spending four weeks in the hospital, most of which lying in bed, my muscles were unbelievably weak. The walk across the parking lot to the pharmacy tired me more than running seven miles. Walking down one flight of stairs tired me more than lifting six hundred and thirty pounds on the leg press. This was a reality check. It would be some time before I would regain my strength.

Colletha and Becky finally came. Colletha drove me over to Wayne and Jacqui's house. After I hobbled up the stairs, one stair at a time, I lay on the bed. It felt so good to lay in a bed other than a hospital bed. I drifted off to sleep looking forward to seeing Nina the next day.

When Nina saw me, she asked why I was still wearing my hospital bracelet? I told her, in jest, that I was wearing it as a memento, not to mention if something happened on the drive to Atlanta. Nina commented that I was not trusting God to totally heal me. I reassured her that it was just a memento and that I would take it off after I was back in Atlanta. However, I was probably subconsciously reflecting on the concerns expressed by my doctors regarding the long drive to Atlanta. They were insistent that I have all of my medical information with me in the event that I required further medical attention during the trip home. While these comments may have caused me to question subconsciously or consciously, it was just a memento.

The next day Nina, Jalani, and me went to visit my friend Greg and his family. While Greg played with Jalani and his two sons, Tyler and Kyle, I soaked in the Jacuzzi. I was scheduled to see Dr. Lewis later that afternoon for my final appointment. Because of some redness in my eyes, I was scheduled to be examined by a retina specialist and have blood testing done before my examination by Dr. Lewis. Dr. Lewis was concerned about any possible bleeding related to the blood thinners I had been taking. The retina specialist found that I had cysts on both of my retinas. While the cysts didn't appear to be infected, he believed that they were related to the infection in my arm. He insisted that I see another retina specialist when I returned to Atlanta. Such an infection could cause blindness!

As if this wasn't enough, I noticed that after I got out of the Jacuzzi, I had developed a slight pain while sitting. It got worse as the day wore on so I mentioned it to Dr. Lewis. He examined me and discovered that I had developed a hemorrhoid. Apparently my journey was not over.

With everything that I had gone through, I thought, "This too shall pass." Nina and I spent the next few days at Wayne and Jacqui's as we prepared for our return trip to Atlanta. Under the guise of visiting family in Alabama, Nina's mother and father returned with us to Atlanta. They really wanted to make sure that I got home and that I didn't die along the way! During the ride, I reflected on the previous weeks in the hospital and I began to appreciate the kindness and prayers of all those who helped or prayed me through it.

I have fought a good fight, I have finished my
course, I have kept the faith.
[2 Timothy 4:7]

On the first day back in Atlanta, Nina and I pondered how we would identify the various doctors needed to continue the healing process. During our discussion, the door bell rang. One of our neighbors, Marsha, had come with a friend, Paige, who was an artist. Paige is a portrait artist and they had come to invite us to see Paige's work at Marsha's home that weekend. Nina shared with them the story of my hospitalization and how we were now searching for local doctors. Paige mentioned that there was a husband and wife team from her church. The wife practiced internal medicine and the husband was a cardiologist. Perfect! Paige called the wife, Dr. Deborah St. Claire, who agreed to see me the next day. This was perfect. I needed to have a blood test done to monitor the Coumadin (blood thinning medication).

Though I walk in the midst of trouble, thou
wilt revive me: thou shalt stretch forth thine
hand against the wrath of mine enemies, and
thy right hand shall save me. The Lord will
perfect that which concerneth me: thy mercy, O
Lord, endureth for ever.
[Psalm 138:7,8]

The next day when Nina and I met with Dr. St. Claire, we welcomed her to our team! She was now doctor number sixteen. I had fun teasing Dr. St. Claire because she was the youngest doctor yet. I asked her, "Are you really a doctor? How long have you been out of medical school? You know all of the doctors that I have seen have been specialists." Nina and I found Dr. St. Claire to be an extraordinary blessing. She was willing to help us find the other specialists that I needed. She made an appointment for me with an infectious disease specialist at Emory University. She also made an appointment for me with her husband, Don, a Cardiologist. Once again, here we were being led into the hands of God's anointed.

I met with Dr. Kozarsky, an infectious disease specialist, who I found to be as personable and as knowledgeable as Dr. Shriner. When I met with Dr. St. Claire's husband, Don, he had another echocardiogram done. It revealed no clotting and no permanent damage to my heart as a result of the heart attack. In fact, Dr. St. Claire told me that there was no evidence, whatsoever, that I had had a heart attack. He also had me take a treadmill test to see how strong my heart was. I not only went through the test with flying colors, but I was able to push the treadmill to a point that he and his nurse had never witnessed. The final diagnosis was that my heart was as strong as it was the day before I went to California and that I could resume my normal workout schedule. Praise God!

Exactly six weeks from the day of my last workout, I returned to the gym. I ran on the treadmill at just under my normal pace for forty-five minutes. Although I still had limited flexibility in my arm, my return to the gym was testimony to God's grace and mercy having brought me full circle. A week later, I conducted three workshops at a conference at the University of Maryland. I wore the same suit, shirt, and tie that I had worn at the conference in California. In my workshop, I shared my testimony, marking a new beginning.

*Put on the new man, which is renewed
in knowledge after the image of Him
that created him.*

[Colossians 3:10]

EPILOGUE

Thank You, Father

For I would that all men were even as I myself.
But every man hath his proper gift of God, one
after this manner, and another after that.
[1 Corinthians 7:7]

I believe that God anointed me to write this book in the second grade when I first became aware of the special gift that He had given me. My unique gift of writing, together with my faith, has allowed me to see past my circumstances to the powerful testimony manifest within my journey.

The anointing which ye have received of
Him abideth in you, and ye need not that
any man teach you: but as the same anointing
teacheth you of all things, and is truth, and
is no lie, and even as it hath taught you, ye
shall abide in Him.
[1 John 2:27]

As I share with the parents and teachers whom I speak to throughout the country, our beliefs and experiences ultimately define what we do. If we do not nurture our children; teach them to believe in the potential and possibilities [faith] in their lives; and provide them with joyous, loving, and successful life experiences, our failure will ultimately be revealed in what they do. As a Christian, I believe in the death and resurrection of Jesus Christ. I believe in the power and authority that He promised. I believe that *all things are possible to him who believes.* This is my faith. This is the rock upon which I stand. My experiences have taught me that steady and diligent pursuit of your dreams reveals potential, possibilities, and new opportunities each day. The proverbial "Pot of Gold" at the end of rainbow is secondary to the joy of the journey. How boring life would be if each day was guaranteed; if we knew tomorrow's outcome before today's journey began.

> *God gave them knowledge and skill in all*
> *learning and wisdom: and Daniel had*
> *understanding in all visions and dreams.*
> [Daniel 1:17]

While your circumstances may be out of your control, you and you alone are in control of your attitude. It is easy to hold onto your faith and to maintain a positive attitude when everything is going right. The test of your character and integrity will come only when you are consumed in darkness and are able to believe in the light. Only then will you have personal testimony to your faith in the grace and mercy of God.

> *The Lord God is a sun and shield: The Lord*
> *will give grace and glory: no good thing will He*
> *withhold from them that walk uprightly.*
> [Psalm 84:11]

God is love God is light. Let Him love you and let His light shine through you!

A Creed Of Faith

Life holds for you no guarantees
 It may be a stairway growing steeper
Yet if you take each step stride after stride
 You'll grow stronger, instead of weaker

You'll have your ups, and you'll have your downs
 And even when you make it through
There may be times you'll feel, you can't go on
 That there's nothing more that you can do

It's during those times of doubting,
 During those moments of great despair
That you must lift your head up to the sky
 Asking for guidance through your prayer

Ask the Lord to give you the strength
 To make it through another day
Stare each of your problems in the face
 Never yielding, and simply say

"I will do the best that I can do
 I won't let anything hold me down
I'll concede the battle, not the war
 I will always come back around

God within me, there is nothing before me
 That can block the way that I must go
The obstacles that lie in my path
 May make the going slow

But I'll never quit, thus, I will not fail
 And in my life you'll always see
That I will give it all that I've got
 I will become the best that I can be!"

© Mychal Wynn

87

Inspirational Poetry By Mychal Wynn

Thank You Father

Thank you Father,
For the brilliance of your light
guiding my way through all adversity
For the depth of your shadow...
...protecting me from evil
...hand
...and strong
...your wisdom
...wer to my prayer

A Creed of Faith

I Am

I am strong
I am gentle
I am proud
I am humble
...confident

Walking In His Light

When all around you move at a different pace
or in different directions
When you have set your sights on goals
beyond the vision of others
When you dare to dream of things
beyond the imagination of others
When you've tired from your battle
having grown weary from your struggles
Go and find a quiet place
to seek council with your Heavenly Father

Trust in Him
for the answers to your questions
and the strength to...

[Note: These verses are taken from the Book, "Don't Quit"]	Qty	Price	Subtotal
#6001 Test of Faith [Book]		9.95	
#6050 Test of Faith [Audio Tape]		9.95	
Laminated 11 x 17 Inspirational Poster: Attach List of Titles		3.50	

Charge your order to Visa ◦ Mastercard ◦
American Express ◦ Discover or enclose a check.   Shipping [Add .50 per item ordered]

Handling $3.50

TOTAL ____

Mail to: **RISING SUN PUBLISHING, Inc. ◦ P.O. Box 70906 ◦ Marietta, GA 30007-0906**
Phone toll-free: **1-800-524-2813** ◦ FAX: **1-770-587-0862** ◦ email: orderdesk@rspublishing.com

NAME _____

ADDRESS_____

CITY _____ STATE _____ ZIP _____

DAY PHONE (____) _____ DATE: _____

❑ A check (payable to Rising Sun Publishing) is enclosed
Charge my: ❑ Visa ❑ Mastercard ❑ American Express ❑ Discover

Account Number   Expiration Date

Signature (required for credit card purchases)

For further information regarding Mychal's availability to personally share his testimony with your church, school, group, or organization, or, for a complete listing of Mychal's other books and materials contact:

Rising Sun Publishing, Inc.
P.O. Box 70906
Marietta, GA 30007-0906
(800) 524-2813/FAX (770) 587-0862
email: info@rspublishing.com or visit our web site at:
http://www.rspublishing.com

If this book has been a blessing to you, share your thoughts with Mychal Wynn via email at:
mychalwynn@rspublishing.com

~ Notes ~

~ Notes ~

~ Notes ~

~ Notes ~

~ Notes ~